DECOLONISATION: THE BRITISH EXPERIENCE
SINCE 1945

UP

Decolonisation:
The British Experience Since 1945

NICHOLAS J. WHITE

LONGMAN
LONDON AND NEW YORK

Addison Wesley Longman Limited,
Edinburgh Gate,
Harlow,
Essex CM20 2JE,
United Kingdom
and Associated Companies throughout the world.

*Published in the United States of America
by Addison Wesley Longman Inc, New York*

First published 1999

ISBN 0-582-29087 2 PPR

Visit Addison Wesley Longman on the world wide web at http://www.awl-he.com

British Library Cataloguing-in-Publication Data
A catalogue record for this book is available from the British Library

Library of Congress Cataloging-in-Publication Data
White, Nicholas J., 1967–
    Decolonisation: the British experience since 1945 / Nicholas J. White
      p. cm.
    Includes bibliographical references (p.   ) and index.
    ISBN 0-582-29087-2
    1. Great Britain--Colonies--History--20th century.
    2. Commonwealth countries--History. 3. Decolonization. I. Title.
DA16.W47   1999
909'.09712410825--dc21   98-40552

Set by 7 in 10/12 Sabon
Printed in Malaysia, PP

CONTENTS

AN INTRODUCTION TO THE SERIES

Such is the pace of historical enquiry in the modern world that there is an ever-widening gap between the specialist article or monograph, incorporating the results of current research, and general surveys, which inevitably become out of date. *Seminar Studies in History* are designed to bridge this gap. The series was founded by Patrick Richardson in 1966 and his aim was to cover major themes in British, European and World history. Between 1980 and 1996 Roger Lockyer continued his work, before handing the editorship over to Clive Emsley and Gordon Martel. Clive Emsley is Professor of History at the Open University, while Gordon Martel is Professor of International History at the University of Northern British Columbia, Canada and Senior Research Fellow at De Montfort University.

All the books are written by experts in their field who are not only familiar with the latest research but have often contributed to it. They are frequently revised, in order to take account of new information and interpretations. They provide a selection of documents to illustrate major themes and provoke discussion, and also a guide to further reading. The aim of *Seminar Studies* is to clarify complex issues without over-simplifying them, and to stimulate readers into deepening their knowledge and understanding of major themes and topics.

NOTE ON REFERENCING SYSTEM

Readers should note that numbers in square brackets [5] refer them to the corresponding entry in the Bibliography at the end of the book (specific page numbers are given in italics). A number in square brackets preceded by *Doc.* [*Doc. 5*] refers readers to the corresponding item in the Documents section which follows the main text. There is a Guide to Main Characters and these are asterisked at first occurrence in the text.

LIST OF MAPS

ABBREVIATIONS

CDC	Colonial Development Corporation
CIS	Commonwealth of Independent States (former Soviet Union)
CD&W	Colonial Development and Welfare
CPP	Convention People's Party (Gold Coast/Ghana)
EEC	European Economic Community
EFTA	European Free Trade Area
FLN	Front de Libération Nationale (Algeria)
GNP	Gross National Product
IMF	International Monetary Fund
MCA	Malayan Chinese Association
MCP	Malayan Communist Party
MPLA	Movimento Popular de Libertação de Angola
NATO	North Atlantic Treaty Organisation
NCNC	National Council of Nigeria and the Cameroons
NLM	National Liberation Movement (Gold Coast/Ghana)
UGCC	United Gold Coast Convention
UMNO	United Malays National Organisation
UN[O]	United Nations Organisation

ACKNOWLEDGEMENTS

I would like to record the support I received from the School of Social Science and the History Section at Liverpool John Moores University in the writing of this book. In particular my colleague, Frank McDonough, deserves special praise. For their patience and good humour, I must also mention the staff of the Inter Library Loans Unit at LJMU. Professor Tony Stockwell of Royal Holloway College and Dr. Rob Holland of the Institute of Commonwealth Studies have been the source of encouragement and ideas over the years.

This book is dedicated to my wife, Jan, who has been an indispensable support and who, in a seminal conversation, inspired the final sentence of this book.

PUBLISHERS' ACKNOWLEDGEMENTS

The publishers would like to thank the following for permission to reproduce copyright material:

Crown copyright is reproduced with the permission of the Controller of Her Majesty's Stationery Office: for extracts from *The Future of Commonwealth Membership*, Report by the Official Committee, 1954, from the *Report of the Commission of Enquiry into Disturbances in the Gold Coast*, 1948, from *The Labour Governments and the End of Empire*, edited by Hyam, 1992, from *The Conservative Governments and the End of Empire* by Goldworthy, 1994, from Cmnd 124 *Defense: Outline of Future Policy*, 1957, and from Cmd 814 *Report of Nyasaland Commission of Enquiry*, 1959. Macmillan Press Ltd for extracts from *Nations and Empires* edited by Bridges *et al*, 1969 and maps from *European Decolonization: An Introductory Survey* by R. F. Holland, 1985; a map from *The British Empire, 1558–1983* by T. O. Lloyd, 1984 by permission of Oxford University Press; Crown copyright material in the Public Record Office is reproduced by permission of the Controller of Her Majesty's Stationery Office: for extracts from PREM 11/1138, Note by Sir Anthony Eden, 28 September 1956 and from FO 371/137972, '*Africa: The Next 10 Years*', December 1959.

PART ONE: INTRODUCTION

1 THE SETTING AND THE PROBLEM

One of the most extraordinary features of postwar international history has been the remarkably rapid disintegration of the British Empire. The empire successfully weathered economic depression and global warfare in the first half of the twentieth century. By the mid-1960s, however, those territories painted red on the map had been reduced to a ramshackle and relatively insignificant set of islands and dependencies. The empire shattered into a set of new, independent nation-states, most of whom found a new relationship of legal equality with Britain within the Commonwealth. In 1973 Britain entered the European Economic Community (later styled European Union), signposting the end of imperial grandeur. The break-up of the empire was the most visible manifestation of contracting British global economic and military power.

Britain's withdrawal from empire can be divided into two main phases. The first phase encompassed the dismantling of Britain's empire in South Asia between 1947 and 1948 – most dramatically involving the independence and fateful partition of India. The British also pulled out of Palestine in this phase. The 'loss' of the rest of the empire did not immediately follow, however, since Africa and Southeast Asia took on new significance for imperial economic and military strategy. The second phase of withdrawal began only in 1957 with independence for the first black African nation south of the Sahara, Ghana. It ended about 1967 as the 'wind of change' blew its path through east and central Africa, the Caribbean and Southeast Asia while Britain's military role 'East of Suez' was also abandoned. A subphase continued through to the 1980s with independence for various Pacific, Indian Ocean, and Caribbean territories and the resolution, for Britain at least, of the Rhodesia/Zimbabwe problem. In 1997 Hong Kong was returned to China.

This is not to say that constitutional change in the empire was neatly confined to the period after the Second World War. After 1931, the so-called 'Dominions' – Australia, Canada, New Zealand, South Africa and the Irish Free State – were legally independent in all internal and external matters. (Although strong economic, military, demographic and emotional ties with Britain remained.) Britain's most important dependency, India, had also received various doses of internal self-government in the course of the twentieth century, culminating in the 1935 Government of India Act which proposed *eventual* self-government for India as a Dominion. This was backed up in 1942 by Britain's promise of postwar independence. Constitutional change in India and the Dominions need not, however, be interpreted as 'imperialism in decline' since such changes were calculated to provide the empire with a new 'streamlined efficiency' [3]. Moreover, at the end of the Second World War, Britain still dominated a vast and various set of territories in Asia, Africa, the West Indies, the Pacific and the Mediterranean where moves towards self-government had hardly begun. It is the dramatic diminution of British imperial authority in the period after 1945 which is the concern of this book.

The book also concerns itself with a region which was not technically part of the empire, but where Britain was still paramount at the end of the Second World War, namely, the Middle East. The most important territories here were Egypt and Iraq which by the 1930s, had achieved legal independence. But 'independence' was subject to Britain retaining effective control over foreign relations and maintaining a military presence because the Suez Canal and the Persian Gulf were regarded as central in defending Britain's imperial interests in Asia and Australasia. The Middle Eastern territories were not colonies, but constituted, instead, an 'informal empire' within the 'imperial system' [5; 16]. As in Africa and Asia, British imperial power disintegrated with startling speed in the postwar Middle East.

The term now employed by historians to describe the process of imperial dissolution for Britain (as well as the other European imperial powers) is decolonisation. On a superficial level, decolonisation describes a definitive constitutional event marking the transfer of political power from the metropolitan country to the new nation state [120]. As midnight struck on 30 to 31 August 1957, for example, the Union Jack was lowered in Kuala Lumpur, the capital of the Federation of Malaya, and the new flag of the independent state was raised. Later on the morning of 31 August a flamboyant independence ceremony was held where British protection over Malaya was formally withdrawn by the Duke of Gloucester (representing the queen), and the new Prime Minister of independent Malaya, Tunku Abdul Rahman*, read out the Proclamation of Independence [189, 3 *p. 467*].

But most historians would regard decolonisation as rather more than the simple lowering and raising of flags at independence ceremonies. Two recent definitions will illustrate this. John Hargreaves in 1988 suggested that decolonisation could be defined as 'the intention to terminate formal political control over specific colonial territories, and to replace it by some new relationship' [10 *p. 2*]. Also in 1988 John Darwin suggested that the process might be defined as 'a partial retraction, redeployment and redistribution of British and European influences in the regions of the extra-European world' [5 *p. 7*]. In both these definitions, then, 'decolonisation' is not necessarily synonymous with the 'end of empire' or 'independence'. British policy-makers at the end of the Second World War did not envisage full independence for their colonial territories. But, in an attempt to revitalise and streamline the empire, Britain did attempt to adjust political relationships; a process which ultimately, it could be argued, accelerated and escalated beyond Britain's control. Decolonisation can thus be seen as a process initiated in London. The next part of this book examines the calculations and recalculations of imperial policy-makers in their attempts to deal with the 'different and harsher climate' that 'opened up after 1945' [5 *p. 17*].

Yet, a focus on the imperial or metropolitan level of analysis might overstate the degree to which the British *chose* to decolonise. In contrast, an 'internal' or 'nationalist' approach to decolonisation would focus on the grass-roots developments in the colonial periphery. Indeed, this might seem a far more attractive means of explaining imperial collapse since economic, political and social changes in colonial societies in the course of the twentieth century – culminating in the rise of mass nationalist movements – ultimately meant that Britain could no longer control its empire in the postwar era. The 'revolting periphery', it would appear, *forced* the British to admit defeat and withdraw unceremoniously from one colonial possession after another. The third part of this book, then, seeks to explain the rise of populist nationalism in the British Empire after the Second World War.

On another level entirely, however, it could be argued that what fundamentally brought about the empire's collapse was the radically changed international political environment after the Second World War. The fourth part of the book thus analyses the degree to which the emergence of two extra-European and nominally anti-imperial superpowers, as well as anti-colonial international institutions such as the United Nations Organisation (UN[O]), squeezed the British out of empire. The final part of the book goes on to assess the British experience in the light of other decolonisations. Generally, the study avoids a blow-by-blow account of decolonisation in the diverse mass of colonial territories which made up the British imperial system. This would be an impossible task in such a concise book and readers are thus encouraged to turn to other longer studies, listed in the bibliography, for more detailed explanations of events in particular territories. Instead, this book is concerned with unravelling the major themes in, and interpretations of, Britain's imperial demise.

PART TWO: IMPERIAL POLICY AND DECOLONISATION

2 LABOUR'S EMPIRE, 1945–1951

1945: THE BEGINNING OF THE END?

Given the weak position of Britain by the end of the Second World War, there is a temptation to regard the decolonisation of the British Empire as an inevitability. Metropolitan crises induced by wartime debt in the 1920s and world slump in the 1930s were exacerbated by the combined onslaught from Germany, Italy and Japan between 1939 and 1945. Britain in contrast to other European imperial powers, such as France, was undefeated in Europe. None the less, the economic costs of total war were apparently too great for Britain to remain a great power in the postwar world. The British war effort had been dependent on massive loans from the United States and the liquidation of overseas assets. This meant that by the end of the global conflict, Britain was overspending its own income by over £2,000 million a year, its industrial machinery was worn out, and its exports had lost two-thirds of their value. The esteemed economist, Lord Keynes, warned in August 1945 of a 'financial Dunkirk' facing peacetime Britain [Doc. 1].

The new Labour government was forced to negotiate a loan from the United States of $3.75 billion. But the Americans attached conditions: sterling would be made fully convertible with the dollar in July 1947. During the Second World War, and in its immediate aftermath, sterling was an inconvertible, 'soft currency'. Hence, any country which traded with Britain could only spend its sterling earnings in Britain or in other countries – principally British colonies and ex-colonies – which linked their currencies to sterling within the economic bloc known as the sterling area (see pp. 7–8). Free sterling-dollar convertibility would allow for the development of a more open world trading system in which countries could convert their sterling earnings into dollars and, hence, purchase American and other dollar-area goods. American economic liberalism thus threatened to strike at the imperial trade preferences and currency controls which had knitted the empire together as an economic unit [42; 130].

In the general election of July 1945 Clement Attlee's* Labour Party triumphed over Winston Churchill's* Conservatives with an over-whelming mandate for domestic renovation and a welfare state. The National Health Service, the expansion of education, council housing, old age pensions, and unemployment insurance on top of the nation-alisation of the economy's commanding heights, placed a fresh set of financial demands on an Exchequer already overburdened by over-seas commitments. Now suffering from an acute case of 'imperial overstretch', Britain, it would seem, could no longer afford a world-wide empire: economic and military assets simply did not match over-seas and domestic liabilities [20; 125].

Alongside severe military and economic strain, British imperialism had faced a huge moral blow during the Second World War. The fall of Singapore to the Japanese in February 1942 has been described as 'the most shattering imperial military defeat since General Cornwal-lis's surrender at Yorktown in 1781' [13 *p. 178*]. It was a shattering psychological defeat too. The British were expelled from Hong Kong, Malaya, Borneo and Burma by a non-European power. In an age when imperial ideology still hinged on claims of European racial superiority, the myth of the invincible white man was exploded over-night. Britain returned to its Far Eastern possessions following the collapse of Japan in August 1945, but clearly political relationships between rulers and ruled would have to change. Another moral pres-sure came from Britain's wartime alliance with the United States. The British imperial record (in the Far East particularly) was subject to intense American criticism [127; 136]. Given Britain's economic, mili-tary and moral weaknesses, burgeoning colonial independence move-ments, it would appear, simply had to apply a little pressure to bring the whole imperial edifice tumbling down.

The British Empire was subject to new stresses and strains after 1945, but the scenario outlined above is too simplistic. Britain may have emerged from the Second World War with limited resources for its worldwide commitments, but British policy-makers did not lack the will to maintain both the empire and Britain's role as a global power. If anything, the empire took on a new significance for Britain in the post-war world. As Ronald Hyam has written 'two quintessential themes dominated the colonial policy of the Labour government between 1945 and 1951: economic recovery and Russian expansion. ... Both problems predicated enhanced interest in the empire in general and Africa in particular' [31 *p. xxiii*].

good quote

Labour did preside over Britain's withdrawal from India and Palestine, but, at the same time, Africa, Southeast Asia and the Middle East were subject to a 'new imperialism'. A curious blend of imperial 'crisis' and imperial 'commitment' characterised the immediate postwar years. The Labour Cabinet contained powerful individuals, such as Prime Minister Attlee and Foreign Secretary Ernest Bevin,* who were determined to defend Britain's extra-European role. Despite the anti-colonial leanings of many Labour Party members, socialist principles were sacrificed to metropolitan self-interest in Labour's colonial policies between 1945 and 1951 [26].

ECONOMICS AND THE NEW IMPERIALISM

Imperial Trade and the Sterling Area

Paradoxically, war-torn exhaustion and relative economic weakness meant that 'more completely than ever before economics and empire had come together' [4 *p. 197*]. As secure markets for British goods, Britain's colonial possessions could offset declining British industrial competitiveness, especially if the largest economy in the world, the United States, chose to retreat behind tariff walls in a repetition of the depressed 1930s. The development of colonial economies would boost the purchasing power of colonial consumers thus helping to compensate British industry for markets lost during the Second World War [11].

Certain colonies were also considered vital as commodity producers which earned urgently needed dollars for the sterling area. The sterling area was formed at the beginning of the war and was made up of most of the empire-Commonwealth. After 1945 it was much more tightly controlled and the area discriminated against trade with 'hard currency' areas, particularly the United States, and became largely a device for dollar earning. Colonial exports, such as rubber from Malaya and cocoa from the Gold Coast, had developed huge markets in the United States and were hence massive dollar earners. Via the three main requirements of the sterling area, however, the colonies were not permitted to spend their dollars freely. Firstly, the colonies based their currencies on sterling and maintained fixed exchange rates with the pound; secondly, Britain bought all the hard currency earned by the colonies, credited them with sterling balances, and in exchange provided an allocation of sterling; and thirdly, the sterling area required colonies to maintain exchange controls against the currencies of non-sterling-area countries, while permitting free sterling transfers inside the area [77 *p. 275*].

Thus the sterling area system maintained the value of the pound by helping the British balance of payments position, and acted as a 'counter-inflationary cushion' at a time when nationalisation and universal social welfare schemes were being established in the United Kingdom [11 *p. 168*]. The system might not have been quite so inequitable had Britain been able and willing to provide the goods which net dollar earners, such as the Gold Coast and Malaya, wished to purchase outside the sterling area. But British manufacturing undercapacity, combined with the priority given to exporting to dollar markets and fears about running down sterling balances, ensured a prolonged shortage of consumer goods which produced inflationary conditions in many colonies throughout the 1940s [26].

It was unlikely that the Labour government would grant wholesale independence for the colonies, especially as London's ability to impose its financial will on independent members of the sterling area (e.g. Australia) became difficult once the war was over. 'In the late 1940s and early 1950s the [colonial] empire was the backbone of the whole sterling area, largely because it was there that Britain could impose monetary and financial policies through political control' [35 *p. 260*] Tight control on colonial monetary policy was also imperative to prevent a rapid run on accumulated colonial sterling balances. This might result in massive destabilisation and inflation in the British economy. Transferring power to colonial nationalists who might draw irresponsibly on the balances was clearly out of the question for the Labour government (and its Conservative successor until at least the mid-1950s) [28].

Colonial Economic Development

The Treasury in London became increasingly attracted to the potentialities of colonial economic development as a strategy to boost colonial exports to the dollar area, particularly following the convertibility crisis of August 1947. Sterling convertibility – a condition of the huge United States loan to Britain in 1945 – had to be suspended when holders of sterling outside Britain swiftly ran down their balances, and Britain was faced with financial ruin. This meant that far from the sterling area being dismantled – a feared consequence of sterling-dollar interconvertibility and American economic liberalism in general – the imperial economy was more tightly controlled than ever before. Only sterling earned by dollar-area countries was convertible; so-called 'transferable' sterling – used to finance trade within the sterling area – remained officially inconvertible. The failure of convertibility forced Britain's dependence on colonial sterling balances and dollar earnings to underwrite the domestic economy. Solving Britain's post-war dollar shortage by stimulating colonial exports to the United States was also a key element in the 1949 decision to devalue the pound by 30 per cent, and the sterling crisis of November 1951 later re-emphasised the integral role of colonial primary producers in British economic recovery [27; 35; 42].

Up to the Second World War, Britain's vast African estate had proved of negligible value despite the mythological treasure chest believed to be buried there. The war years, however, witnessed the rise of a more intrusive economic imperialism and this was to be carried on by the Attlee government in peacetime as British colonial administrations sought to stimulate and regulate the production of raw materials considered to be of value to the metropolitan economy [8]. Sir Stafford Cripps,* Minister for Economic Affairs, told a conference of African governors in November 1947 that with the sterling area's dollar deficit running at £600 to £700 millions a year 'we should increase out of all recognition the tempo of African economic development' boosting production of anything 'that will save dollars or will sell in a dollar market' [*Doc. 2*].

Oil and cotton from the maze of protectorates, allied and protected states, and mandated territories that made up Britain's empire in the Middle East were also vital for UK economic recovery and future prosperity. In 1949, an official committee in Britain hoped that by 1951 some 82 per cent of Britain's oil would be extracted from the Middle East, representing the 'largest single factor in balancing Britain's overseas payments' [16 *p. 18*]. The loss of oil production in Iran following the nationalisation of the British-owned Abadan refinery in 1951 was more than compensated for by the growth of output from the British-protected states in the Gulf, especially Kuwait.

The 1940s were littered with state-led development projects aimed at harnessing the economic potential of the colonial empire. The most ambitious was the notorious East African Groundnuts Scheme. The initial proposal in 1946 was for one million acres to be cultivated in Tanganyika. This was presented as a solution to the world-wide shortage of edible oils and fats for a Labour government which had to cope with the twin problems of food scarcities and a shortage of hard currency to purchase imports. The scheme was approved by the Cabinet in January 1947 and was taken over by the newly established Overseas Food Corporation in April 1948 [7; 15, 2]. Groundnuts ranks as the archetypal failure of British postwar colonial development (see Chapter 3, p. 26). But, wastefulness aside, development projects like groundnuts, or the production of eggs in Gambia, clearly illustrate the new imperial spirit in London.

Futter development of Crupps ideas

To facilitate economic development in the colonies, the Colonial Development Corporation (CDC) – with borrowing powers of up to £100 million – was formed in London in 1948 [21]. Colonial Secretary, Arthur Creech Jones,* informed Attlee that the CDC would 'promote in every possible way increased colonial production on an economic and self-supporting basis with an eye to the production of foodstuffs, raw materials and manufactures whose supply to the UK or sale overseas will assist our balance of payments' [33 *p. 132*]. Heightened interest in the economic potentials of the empire is also emphasised by the creation of the Cabinet's Colonial Development Committee at the end of 1948 [31]. A more interventionist stance was also facilitated by the vast increase in the staffing strength of the Colonial Office by 45 per cent between 1945 and 1954. Although a weak entity compared with the Foreign Office and the Treasury, the Colonial Office still 'enjoyed in these years an excitement and an economic initiative unknown since the days of the Boer War' [40 *p. 201*]. In 1945, the Colonial Office succeeded in securing from the Treasury £120 million pounds for the colonies through the new Colonial Development and Welfare Act. This greatly expanded upon the previous provisions of 1929 and 1940 [7; 15, 2]. *Did do some good for colonies but few and far between*

Economic exploitation was not the only motive in Britain's new development thrust into the colonial empire. There was an altruistic and idealistic component which sought genuinely to raise colonial standards of living, and emphasis was continually placed on the mutual benefits which both Britons and colonial peoples would derive from overseas development. Yet, as the metropole's economic crisis deepened, especially after 1947, the Colonial Office's vision of colony-centred, welfarist development as a prelude to self-government gave way to the Treasury's penchant for maximum primary production for export to the dollar area and the Board of Trade's desire to uphold markets for metropolitan manufactures in the colonies [22].

The new development initiative – whether exploitative or welfarist – required a significant expansion in local bureaucracies, and the period after 1945 witnessed a fresh invasion of British and Commonwealth personnel to fill expanding technical departments overseas: between June 1945 and September 1948 alone the Colonial Service attracted some 4,100 new recruits [20 *p. 104*]. The term 'second colonial occupation' has been used to describe this phenomenon in postwar Africa [37], but it can equally be applied to Southeast Asia and the Caribbean as well as Britain's informal empire in the Middle East.

→ Reason for failure and eventual decolonisation

GLOBAL STRATEGY, PRESTIGE AND THE NEW IMPERIALISM

The new age of British imperialism after 1945 was more than economic in tone. British strategists in the late 1940s and early 1950s had hardly accepted a limited European role. For Bevin and his Foreign Office advisors, at least, 'British weakness was a temporary rather than a permanent phenomenon' [33 *p. 77*]. Attlee and his Cabinet had not accepted the *Pax Americana* especially as a chief aim of Washington's Marshall Aid Plan for European recovery (launched in the summer of 1947) was to foster Western Europe's transformation into an integrated economic community in which Britain would substitute leadership in Europe for its imperial world role. The rejuvenation of the empire and the Commonwealth thus emerged for the Labour government as a central means of circumventing American designs for Britain to reinvent itself as merely the regional leader of Western Europe [11; 42]. Attlee, in a style befitting Lord Salisbury or Joseph Chamberlain, declared to parliament in 1948 that 'we are not solely a European power, but a member of a great Commonwealth and Empire' [187, 1 *p. 59*].

The 'Third Force'

The 'new imperialism' was a means of Britain continuing to play an independent, global role in the world. British postwar leaders were committed to creating a 'third force' in world politics – the idea of expanding Britain's power to equal the United States and the Soviet Union. This could be achieved by combining the resources of Western Europe, the Dominions, and the Afro-Asian colonies under British leadership [51 *p. 319*]. According to Bevin: 'we have the material resources in the Colonial Empire, if we develop them, and by giving a spiritual lead now we should be able to carry out our task in a way which will show clearly that we are not subservient to the United States of America or to the Soviet Union' [*Doc. 3*]. In October 1948 Bevin famously opined that 'if we only pushed on and developed Africa, we could have the US dependent on us, and eating out of our hands in four or five years. ... The US is very barren of essential materials, and in Africa we have them all' [31 *p. l; 32 p. 179*].

Among Bevin's more fantastic plans was the creation of a British-led Western Union; a democratic alliance encompassing the whole of Western Europe. In this, the African colonial resources of the other European imperial powers (France, Portugal, Belgium and Spain) would be pooled with those of Britain as a vital element in building up British power [31; 32; 33] [*Doc. 3*]. The 'Euro-Africa' concept would effectively entail France and the lesser Western European powers becoming (in John Kent's phrase) '"collaborators" with the British Empire' [33 *p. 62*]. In the short term, the Western Union might be supported by the Americans, but Bevin ultimately 'wanted to design a European system that would extend to Africa and the Middle East rather than across the Atlantic'. The long-term aim was thus to 'break free' from dependence on the United States [33 *p. 161*]. Certainly, considerable efforts were made at colonial co-operation with France, in particular, on matters such as education, health, transport and labour [33; 166].

However, the massive sterling devaluation and the explosion of an atomic bomb by the Soviet Union in the course of 1949 exposed the fundamental weakness of the British international position. Ministers were persuaded that Euro-Africa should be abandoned. Instead, the Western Union was transmuted into the concept of the Atlantic alliance (i.e. to include the United States). The 'special relationship' with the United States was now viewed as 'vital to preserve the Empire' [33 *p. 202*]. In April 1949, Britain joined the American-led North Atlantic Treaty Organization (NATO) as the best means of fending off Soviet aggression in Europe. Even so, empire and Commonwealth remained in British international strategy as a means of avoiding complete subservience to the United States and, hence, the assumption of a purely European role [5; 11; 12].

The Military and Strategic Value of Africa

In the grand, global thinking of the 1940s and 1950s, Africa was not merely an economic surrogate for India. The continent might also serve as the basis for a new imperial army to replace the Indian army which in its heyday had been deployed throughout the British Empire. Field Marshall Bernard Montgomery (Chief of the Imperial General Staff) toured Africa in 1947 and, in a report hopelessly optimistic and insensitive to colonial realities, believed he had stumbled upon an untapped and potentially huge military resource [32; 33]. In 1950 it was estimated that Africa could provide 400,000 troops for an imperial army [31 *p. lx*]. A new major military base was also proposed in east Africa as a possible alternative to Palestine [30]. Like the African army, this did not come to full fruition. Nor did plans for a transcontinental road or rail link from Lagos to Mombasa or for the emigration of British populaces and industries to reduce metropolitan vulnerability in a Soviet atomic attack [30; 33]. But in the atmosphere of the late-1940s anything seemed possible in the colonial field.

The Strategic Value of the Middle East

Britain's informal empire in the Middle East, as Bevin told the Cabinet in August 1949, was 'strategically ... a focal point of communications, a source of oil, a shield to Africa and the Indian Ocean, and an irreplaceable offensive base' [36 *p. 16*]. Britain's military strength, as well as its balance of payments, depended upon supplies of Middle Eastern oil [16]. Given the costs of reconstruction in the immediate aftermath of war and the advent of air power, Attlee had argued for a strategic withdrawal from the Middle East; military resources should be concentrated on defending the sea lanes round the Cape to the Far East and Australia as a cheaper and safer substitute for the route through the Mediterranean and the Suez Canal. Attlee's strategy of Middle-Eastern disengagement, however, was rejected by Bevin, the Foreign Office and the military top-brass. Britain must continue its traditional defence role in the region as a means of containing Russia; the Middle-Eastern vacuum formed by withdrawal from the Mediterranean route would swiftly be filled by the Soviets. Russian infiltration of the Middle East would, in turn, threaten Britain's new economic empire in Africa [16; 31; 33].

The Middle East was also central to imperial defence planning because Britain's fleet of heavy bombers lacked the range to strike at the heart of the Soviet Union, except from bases in the Middle East [16; 24]. Like Africa, the Middle East was also one region of the world 'where the Americans, it was fondly supposed, could be manoeuvred and if necessary blackmailed, into following the British wake, rather than *vice versa*' [13 *p. 347*]. The victory of Bevin's imperial strategy meant that by the late 1940s, the British presided over military installations in Egypt, Palestine, Iraq, Jordan, the Sudan, Bahrain and Aden.

The Middle East, then, remained 'the hub of strategic defence planning' [31 *p. lviii*]. Britain's new imperialism in the region is evinced by the establishment of a new base in the ex-Italian territory of Cyrenaica. This spacious and sparsely populated area could have been ideal for the British atomic weapons programme (finally approved by a secret Cabinet sub-committee in January 1947) [36]. With the loss of Palestine in 1948 the British were determined to remain in the Canal Zone in Egypt, while uncertainty about the long-term British future in Suez gave military installations in Cyprus greater centrality. A regional defence pact was Britain's ultimate design. This would deal with the twin problems of containing the Soviet Union and over-reliance on the United States [36; 144].

The Military and Strategic Value of the Far East

Although regarded as less important by planners than the Middle East, Britain's strategic role in the Far East was equally undiminished after 1945. As a result of American pressure during the war, the Foreign Office accepted that Britain might have to give up its colonial possessions in East and Southeast Asia as part of a general strategy to harmonise relations with the United States. But that attitude was gradually changed towards the end of the war; increasingly the retention of Far Eastern territories was seen as a matter crucial to the retention of global power [33; 46; 50]. Despite withdrawal from the Indian Empire, the British did not significantly reappraise their traditional military role 'East of Suez' [25]. In the cost-cutting atmosphere of the immediate postwar years, the Attlee government looked forward to a drastic scaling down of British naval commitments in the Far East. But, with the spread of the Cold War to Asia (particularly after communist China's intervention in the Korean war at the end of 1950), Southeast Asia came to be seen as a vital strategic link between the United Kingdom, Africa, and Australasia. As a result, funds were poured into the Singapore naval base and it flourished as never before [41].

Indeed, Singapore replaced Delhi as British headquarters in Asia, and became 'a centre for the radiation of British influence' [46 *p. 86*]. From June 1948 Malaya was a frontline state in the Cold War following the outbreak of communist insurrection there; a costly colonial war would be fought to secure Malaya against communist takeover. A general aim of British policy was to establish a Southeast Asian regional organisation under British leadership to contain Soviet influence and so preserve British commercial and political interests. This bore fruit in the Commonwealth's Colombo Plan, launched in January 1950, to improve living standards in Southeast Asia and, hence, to reduce the attractions of communism [46; 49; 50].

The British also reasserted their position in Northeast Asia: Hong Kong, alongside its perceived commercial value, had an enhanced strategic role to play in the Cold War following the victory of the communists in the Chinese civil war by the end of 1949. For British strategists, if Hong Kong was left to China, communist takeovers could follow in Southeast Asia and India [31; 51; 53].

POLITICAL CHANGE AND THE NEW IMPERIALISM

British policy-makers did recognise that in order to preserve the benefits and the potentials of empire intact, political relationships between coloniser and colonised would have to change. As a means to effective exploitation, Labour's new imperialism also contained a strategy of political reform in the colonial 'periphery'.

Political Advance

Senior civil servants in the Colonial Office, in particular, were conscious 'of the need for a clear policy based on the political advancement' of colonial peoples [30 *p. 150*] [*Doc. 4*]. Three main reasons for this stand out. Firstly, an element of self-government would meet African and Asian nationalist aspirations which had been stimulated by the war. Secondly, political development in the colonies would pre-empt international pressures from the United States, the United Nations and enlightened world opinion to dismantle the empire; an image of progressive imperialism would be presented to the world. Thirdly, the wider participation of colonial peoples was the crucial 'political instrument' required for stimulating social and economic development [30 *p. 150*]. Increasing non-European stakeholders in the imperial enterprise would enhance the empire's efficiency and its propensity for effective exploitation for metropolitan benefit. At the same time, meeting the demands of Asian, Arab and African nationalism through opening up local and central government, as well as the administration, to indigenous participation was a key element in the international policy of blocking Soviet imperialism. From 1948, British colonial policy was increasingly directed at isolating potentially pro-Soviet 'extremists' through promoting moderate, non-communist colonial nationalists into government. Here 'was the only sure way to preserve the long-term friendship and goodwill of former colonies on which future trading and strategic facilities and continuing membership of the Commonwealth [and thus of the Western alliance] would ultimately depend' [31 *p. xxix*].

In all this, the central plank of prewar colonial administration – indirect rule – was to be modified. 'Indirect rule' was a policy adopted by the British in Africa (although it found informal echoes in the Middle East and Southeast Asia) towards the plethora of chiefs, sultans, emirs and kings who inhabited the empire. The policy was given formal expression by the African administrator, Lord Lugard, in *The Dual Mandate in Tropical Africa*, first published in 1922. The prime aim of British administration was, wherever possible, to rule through traditional native rulers under the guidance and control of British officials. This was a conservative method of colonial governance which excluded the African middle class from political power to preserve the local authority and, hence, 'collaboration' of the traditional chiefs and rulers [48; 107].

Indirect rule was a classic device for ruling cheaply and efficiently with limited British personnel. By the 1930s, however, the system was under attack. Lord Hailey, Director of the African Research Survey, published his important book *An African Survey* in 1938, highlighting the politically antiquated nature of indirect rule which, he claimed, held back urgently needed economic and social modernisation, as well as the development of Westminster-style parliamentary institutions in the colonies. By the 1940s, it is suggested, Hailey's critique had been accepted by the Colonial Office which rejected the traditional chiefs and rulers and looked instead to the Western-educated African intelligentsia as the agents of economic development and nation-building [45]. Much of Labour's colonial reform policy was thus the product of prewar and wartime planning, particularly under the dynamic colonial secretaryships of Malcolm MacDonald* and Oliver Stanley [179, 1].

The implementation of political change in Africa after 1945 was presided over in London by a partnership between a politician and a senior civil servant: Arthur Creech Jones, Labour's Colonial Secretary from 1946 to 1950, and Andrew Cohen,* the left-wing head of the Africa division in the Colonial Office. Both had been heavily influenced by the gradualist-socialist think-tank on colonial affairs, the Fabian Colonial Bureau. As circumstances permitted in each territory, a controlled and orderly transfer of power was envisaged. This would entail a staged progression through elected local government, to elected majorities in central legislative assemblies, to final cabinet government on the Westminster model. These revolutionary plans ran into opposition from 'old guard' colonial officials, but without the transfer of power to educated elites, Cohen and Creech Jones believed that the British would increasingly lose control over African political change [30; 31; 45; 47]. As F. J. Pedler in the Colonial Office believed in 1946, 'a vigorous policy of African local government' would prevent 'the masses' following 'the leadership of demagogues who want to turn us right out very quickly' [*Doc. 4*].

Certainly, the Cohen-Creech Jones partnership presided over major constitutional initiatives, particularly in west Africa. Following riots in the Gold Coast in February 1948 the Coussey Committee of enquiry recommended considerable political advance, and in 1950 a fresh constitution guaranteed an African majority in the legislative council. Kwame Nkrumah's* Convention People's Party won a sweeping election victory in the first elections held in 1951, and for the first time African ministers shared power with European colonial officials in a system known as 'dyarchy' [105; 106]. 'The Gold Coast was well on the way to complete independence [achieved finally in

1957] by the time Labour left office' [40 *p. 204*]. Similar developments followed throughout British Africa (although in eastern and southern Africa, where there were significant white settler populations, constitutional advance lagged behind the west) [40].

A radical rejection of 'indirect rule' was also proposed in Southeast Asia. Before the war, the British were in the Malay states only as the protecting power: the Anglo-Malay treaties from 1874, in return for the institution of 'government by advice', bound Britain to recognise the sovereignty of the sultans and the autonomy of their states. The Malayan Union scheme, devised during wartime and implemented in 1946 following the British return to the peninsula after the Japanese occupation, aimed to create a defensible constitutional unit in which the authority of the sultans was usurped by the colonial government. Meanwhile, a common citizenship would grant equal status with the 'indigenous' Malays to the large Chinese and Indian immigrant communities. *Eventual* self-government was the plan, but the Malayan Union was a means of retaining control of an area of increasing economic and strategic importance to the empire. Malays, fearful of being submerged by the Chinese and the Indians, rallied around their threatened sultans with the result that in 1948 a Federation of Malaya was created which returned some autonomy to the states under a federal central government. Yet, British objectives were still satisfied in that Malaya had a strong central government and the prospect of a single Malayan citizenship [48; 49; 50]. In the summer of 1950 Britain's Commissioner-General in Southeast Asia, Malcolm MacDonald, persuaded Labour Cabinet ministers that Malayan independence should be achieved in fifteen years and moderate Malayan nationalists should be nurtured. This acceleration of political development would allow Britain to retain the initiative in Malaya and throughout Asia [189, 2 *Doc. 218*].

The rejuvenation and prolongation of the British presence in the Middle East also required political changes: formal colonial rule and unequal treaties would be replaced by 'equal' partnerships. Britain would build up goodwill by confirming the political independence of the Middle Eastern states, underpinned by ambitious programmes of economic and social development for 'peasants, not pashas' (in Bevin's phrase). Alliances would thus be developed with a new breed of moderate nationalists in order to prevent the initiative passing to Soviet-backed or -influenced extremists [36]. The British Middle East Office, established in the aftermath of the Second World War, aimed to channel economic aid to the Middle East in an attempt to gain the allegiance of the region's new class of young, progressive politicians and civil servants [34]. Henceforth, British economic and strategic interests would be maintained by co-operation and 'partnership' rather than by old-style imperialism [36].

Political advancement – particularly in Africa – was always conceived by the British as a limited, gradual process smoothly presided over by the colonial authorities. British colonial policy aimed 'to guide the Colonial Territories to responsible self-government within the Commonwealth in conditions that ensure to the people concerned both a fair standard of living and freedom from oppression from any quarter' [*Doc. 5*]. Self-government was the ultimate goal, but self-government was considered far distant. Premature withdrawal would only result in anarchy, Soviet subversion, dictatorship and the loss of British influence, and some smaller territories – for example, Cyprus – were not expected to achieve complete autonomy [30; 31] [*Doc. 5*]

Typical of Labour's strategy for Africa was the Local Self-Government Despatch of 1947 which, it was hoped, would concentrate the energies of African politicians simply on local institutions; an imperial tactic tried, if not tested, in prewar India. The aim was to divert nationalist attentions away from the centre of power to local councils thereby securing the essentials of empire firmly in the hands of British officials [8]. Political change was to be encouraged, but not change that would disrupt economic and strategic relations between metropole and periphery. The pace of change in the Gold Coast (and other African territories with overwhelmingly black populations such as Nigeria) was far faster than expected. None the less, it was hoped that by bringing nationalist politicians like Nkrumah into government, the British could preside over smooth and orderly transfers of power in which British influence and interests would be retained. The alternative was '[b]loody revolution', as Labour's Colonial Secretary, James Griffiths, told a protesting white Kenyan in 1951 [47 *p. 8*].

The New Commonwealth

A key element in Labour's strategy of colonial political change was certainly long term: the creation of a multiracial Commonwealth to preserve British world economic and political influence. The Commonwealth was a free association of self-governing states linked together by common cultural, economic, and strategic interests. Commonwealth membership in the past had served as an effective mechanism for preserving British economic and strategic interests in the 'white' Dominions whose full equality and independence within the Commonwealth had been confirmed by the Statute of Westminster in 1931. For example, Canada, Australia, New Zealand, South Africa, though not Eire (the former Irish Free State), had rallied to the motherland's cause in the Second World War. At the end of the war, Commonwealth membership remained restricted to Britain and the Dominions. The system was constitutionally soldered together by a common allegiance to the British Crown (except the Republic of Eire which, since 1936, had accepted the king only as a diplomatic convenience; and Eire was to leave the Commonwealth in 1949).

The Commonwealth remained after 1945 as a vital element in Britain's aspirations to world-power status, and both British and Dominion leaders were reluctant to disturb the 'club atmosphere' – 'which had been cemented by close co-operation during the Second World War' – by admitting more members. Indeed, it was thought possible to create a two-tier Commonwealth whereby newly-independent Asian and African states would not be admitted as full Commonwealth members. (A particular problem was believed to be the sharing of American strategic intelligence – and discussions of the Cold War generally – with non-whites [69 *pp. 245–7*]).

But, as political change engulfed the empire, a number of changes had to be made by the Attlee government to the nature and membership of the Commonwealth. The principal modification followed India's achievement of independence in 1947 and its expressed desire to become a republic by 1949. As a republic, India necessarily could not recognise the British monarch as Head of State, and, meanwhile, any attempt to create an inferior form of associated membership in the Commonwealth would be resented. In the context of the Cold War, and Bevin's desire to build up British power to rival the United States and the Soviet Union, the Commonwealth needed to be as large as possible. For Attlee, India had to be retained within the Commonwealth. The Chiefs of Staff agreed since this was a means of preventing India from drifting towards the Soviet Union. Hence, membership criteria were modified in 1949 to permit the presence of republics: the king would become head of the new Commonwealth which consisted of both Crown Dominions (in which he would also be king) and Republican Dominions (in which he would not be king) [39; 69 *pp. 248–50*].

The Indian case provided the model for the 1950s and 1960s when many more African and Asian republics rolled off the Commonwealth assembly line. Newly independent ex-colonies would join the multiracial Commonwealth thus creating a 'circle of democratic nations exerting a powerful stabilising influence in the world' [*Doc. 5*]. Commonwealth membership was seen by the Labour government as an important weapon in preventing the growth of communism, as well as maintaining the sterling area.

The Federations

Meanwhile, the British exhibited a constitutional mania for federating groups of colonial territories into larger and stronger political units to facilitate economic development, create strategic power-blocs, prepare the political and administrative ground for the *eventual* transfer of power and reduce the vulnerability of small states to communist takeover.

So the Malayan Union/Federation would be extended to absorb Singapore and the Borneo territories to form the 'Dominion of Southeast Asia' [49; 50]. It was hoped that an East African Federation might bind together Uganda, Tanganyika and Kenya, balancing white settler demands for self-government with the political advancement of the African elite [54]. Similar motives lay behind the Central African Federation – finally inaugurated in 1953 under the Conservative government and encompassing Southern Rhodesia, Northern Rhodesia and Nyasaland. The Federation would also serve as a barrier to the expansion of white South Africa, especially by checking Afrikaner immigration [29]. To create a government capable of planning and mobilising resources over the numerous islands, islets and mainland colonies that made up the British Caribbean, federation was endorsed in 1947 and finally became a reality, again under a Conservative administration, in 1958 [5; 187, 1 and 2].

The majority of these grand plans would unceremoniously crash on the rocks of local political particularisms, most notably in Central Africa. But 'the federations' all illustrate an imperial desire to refashion empire and, in so doing, 'strengthen', rather than weaken, 'the British connection' with overseas dependencies [187, 1 p. 375].

INDIA, PALESTINE AND THE NEW IMPERIALISM

In this new era of imperialism, why did the Attlee government withdraw from India and Palestine between 1947 and 1948 (at the price of partition in both territories)?

The Independence and Partition of India

In the case of India, it could be argued that the Labour government had little choice since the sub-continent had made considerable progress towards self-government before the war. The 1935 Government of India Act conceded that India would *eventually* attain dominion status *à la* Australia, Canada, etc. Moreover, under the new constitution introduced in 1937 the main nationalist party, the Indian National Congress, controlled the governments in a majority of the

Indian provinces. At the centre, however, the British Viceroy continued to maintain a tight grip on India's defence and foreign policy under-pinned by the British-commanded army and police [5 *p. 28*]. The war disrupted and complicated any smooth transfer of power. In 1939, Congress ministers resigned from government in protest at India's inclusion in the war with Germany without Indian consent. This was followed in 1942 by Congress's 'Quit India' campaign. 'Quit India' was effectively suppressed and Congress leaders spent the rest of the war in prison. But, on coming to office in 1945, the Labour govern-ment was 'pledged to honour' the Churchill coalition's offer of post-war independence. This meant postwar elections for a constituent assembly which would then frame a new Indian constitution. 'In return for swift transfer of power, Labour hoped to establish a friendly successor government [within the Commonwealth]' [44 *p. 170*].

The obsolescence of imperial plans was exposed by the realities of Indian politics; in particular, the rivalries between Gandhi's* and Nehru's* Hindu-dominated Congress and Jinnah's* Muslim League. It is debatable if the League's leadership were ever fully committed to a separate Muslim state, Pakistan. But, certainly from 1940, Jinnah was publicly speaking of the impossibility of Hindus and Muslims living together in an independent India. Jinnah, in contrast to Gandhi and Nehru, had strengthened his hand by co-operating with the Brit-ish during the war.

A united and federal India would have been Labour's ideal out-come of independence; British strategic requirements for access to bases, airfields and manpower would thus be secured. Hence, in 1946 a Labour Cabinet Minister, Sir Stafford Cripps, proposed a federation of the Indian provinces in which foreign affairs, defence, communica-tions and finance would be controlled by the federal centre. The pro-posals soon proved unworkable principally because the League feared that Congress sought a more centralised constitution in which the Muslim voice would be muffled. The League announced a policy of direct action to achieve the creation of Pakistan, and in communal rioting in Calcutta during August 1946 over five thousand people died [44 *p. 175*].

At the end of 1946, Cabinet ministers ruled out the possibility of any last-ditch attempt to hold on to India [*Doc. 6*]. In February 1947, with intensified communal violence and the refusal of the League to co-operate in constitution-making, Attlee announced June 1948 as a date for British withdrawal regardless of any League–Congress agree-ment. (It was hoped, however, that fixing a date for independence would force Congress and the League into co-operation.) At the same time, the Viceroy, Wavell, was to be replaced by Lord Louis Mountbatten [44 *pp. 177–8*].

Increasingly independent from London, Mountbatten attempted to win over Congress and the League to an all-India federation. This was rejected by Congress President, Nehru, who feared that, unless a strong centre was maintained, the transfer of power to provinces would merely 'Balkanize' India and lead to further communal disorder. Following another attempt at compromise, Mountbatten too abandoned federation in favour of partition into two separate Dominions; a *fait accompli* regrettably accepted by Attlee's Cabinet in May 1947. In return for accepting partition, Congress demanded a rapid transfer of power. Labour ministers were only contented by Dominion status within the Commonwealth as the price for independence for India and Pakistan in August 1947 [38; 44; 86]. Since they were immediately embroiled in conflict over the partition of Kashmir, neither of the new Dominions were able to participate in Britain's defence plans 'east of Suez'. Independence and partition were also achieved with no guarantees for the minorities (particularly the Sikhs) or Britain's traditional allies, the princes [44]. Swift transfers of power followed in the *Raj*'s adjuncts, Burma and Ceylon, in 1948.

Withdrawal from Palestine

British plans for the Palestine mandate ran up against the competing claims of Jewish and Arab nationalism, as well as the intervention of the United States. Britain's White Paper of 1939 had shocked Zionist leaders because it aimed to cap the Jewish population of Palestine at one-third of the Arab majority. After the war, Bevin attempted to stand firm: the solution to the psychological and refugee problems created by the Holocaust should be resolved by reintegrating the European Jews into Europe. The British would not admit more than 1,500 Jews a month to Palestine. This was in opposition to Zionist thinking which looked forward to mass immigration into Palestine and the creation of a Jewish homeland there. For the British, however, the establishment of a Jewish national state would alienate the Arabs whose goodwill was vital for Britain's wider economic and strategic plans in the Middle East *as a whole* [36]. Bevin was 'pursuing a grand Imperial strategy in which Palestine played only a small but most irritating part' [36 *p. 4*].

However, in August 1945 the President of the United States, Harry S. Truman, suggested the admission of 100,000 Jewish refugees into Palestine. The Labour government feared that this concession would be the thin end of the wedge; opening up Palestine to unlimited Jewish immigration and thus bringing about Arab-Jewish conflict rather than conciliation. The British proposed instead the creation of a joint commission to study the issue. The Anglo-American Committee of Inquiry recommended a bi-national state [36]. But Jewish and Arab nationalists increasingly agitated against any such solution. Jewish groups campaigned for the scrapping of all immigration controls while Arab nationalists demanded a stop to the Jewish diaspora. The actions of Jewish terrorists – such as the bombing of the King David Hotel in Jerusalem in August 1946 – were bogging the British government and military down in a costly and unpopular counter-guerrilla war [36].

After the collapse of the Anglo-American committee's plans, Truman, concerned about the Jewish vote in the United States, increasingly fell into line with the Zionists. In February 1947, the British referred the Palestine issue to the United Nations where it was hoped to win international support for an independent and bi-national state. But the Special Committee recommended partition into Jewish and Arab zones [36]. Bevin wished to have nothing to do with the implementation of the UN plan because British forces might be engaged in 'suppressing Arab resistance' and 'thus antagonising the Arab states' on whose friendship and co-operation rested British paramountcy in the Middle East [5 *p. 120*]. Hence, in September 1947, the Cabinet agreed that the British military and civil administration would be withdrawn in mid-1948 [23; 36; 43] [*Doc. 7*]. The Palestine issue was left to be resolved by the war, which followed British departure, in which some 700,000 Arabs were forced to flee from Jewish-controlled Palestine [36]. The Jewish nation-state, Israel, was then established in 1949.

Imperial Rationalisation

Britain's decisions to quit India and Palestine were not intended to mark the end of empire. Withdrawal was a kind of imperial rationalisation: India and Palestine would be given up (although India and Pakistan were retained within the Commonwealth) while tropical Africa, Southeast Asia, and other parts of the Middle East would be taken up [8; 11].

Given Britain's postwar economic crisis and the fresh demands of the welfare state there was nothing to be gained from expending money and manpower in problem overseas territories. As Holland tells us: 'amidst all the twists and turns of events "on the ground", the Attlee administration, locked into a metropolitan crisis concerned with balancing the demands of social reform and economic stabilization, can be discerned cutting adrift from dependencies which were net liabilities and maintaining a grip on those ... possessions which remained bankable assets' [11 *p. 169*]. Africa, according to Gallagher, 'would be a surrogate for India, more docile, more malleable, more pious' [8 *p. 146*]. According to Cain and Hopkins, India by 1947 'had ceased to be an imperial asset. As far as visible trade was concerned India was now in deficit with the United States and was no longer a net contributor to the Sterling Area's hard currency pool' [2 *p. 196*]. While, in Palestine, 'there could be no question of expending hard-pressed British resources to enforce a settlement against the wishes of both parties' [31 *p. xxvi*]. Moreover, as Bevin told the Cabinet in September 1947, continued involvement in the Palestine dispute would damage Britain's wider interests in the Arab world [*Doc. 7*]. Thus, despite a long-standing, although ill-defined, commitment to Indian independence and Zionist connections within the Labour Party, the withdrawals from South Asia and the Middle East were calculated to assist in the Attlee government's wider designs for global power and influence.

At the same time, the granting of independence in South Asia was not necessarily equated with the end of British influence there. The Attlee government stumbled upon the concept of a new multiracial Commonwealth as a means of supporting Britain's role as a great power: independence within the Commonwealth would enable decolonised states to play a positive role in Commonwealth defence and the sterling area. After 1945 Labour attempted, without success, to obtain formal defence commitments from India as the price of independence. The British would have wished for an arrangement similar to that agreed with Ceylon before independence: in November 1947 Britain was guaranteed continued access to military bases on the island [26; 181, 2] [*Doc. 5*]. Yet as consolation, India – in contrast to Burma which became an independent republic outside the Commonwealth in 1948 – was able to remain within the Commonwealth when it became a republic in 1949. Here was established an enduring facet of British postwar foreign policy; the Commonwealth ideal as an alternative to complete association with either the United States or Europe.

3   SHIFTING PERSPECTIVES? THE 1950s AND THE 1960s

'DISENGAGEMENT'

It has been argued that Britain's new commitment to empire after 1945 was remarkably short-lived [2; 11; 12]. A 'disengagement' took place in the course of the 1950s and 1960s between Britain and its overseas possessions. This was not brought about by imperial weakness. Rather, decolonisation represented a shift in British economic interests from formal empire to the higher-growth regions of Europe and North America. With the return to 'normality' in the international economy in the 1950s, the new emphasis was on trade and investment *between* the industrialised economies to the detriment of colonial primary producers.

Economic trends coalesced with Britain's shifting strategic interests: the new world dominated by the superpowers (the United States and the Soviet Union) increasingly exposed the military redundancy of colonial empires. The possession of a nuclear capability, not an empire, was clearly the modern means to military greatness. Under this argument, the British were not kicked out of empire by the force of colonial protest. Rather, imperial withdrawal followed on logically from the reassessments and recalculations of politicians, officials, military strategists, industrialists and financiers in the metropole [2; 11; 12].

Despite awareness of the growing mismatch between overseas commitments and economic capacity, the empire remained highly prized by the Conservative governments of Winston Churchill and Anthony Eden* between 1951 and 1957. The Tories continued Labour's policies of extended political evolution in the colonies and showed a determination to 'keep change within bounds' [62; 63]. But, by the time of Harold Macmillan's* accession to the premiership in 1957, underlying changes ensured that 'after 1960 ... UK dependencies found themselves hustled towards independence as if the old concerns with "viable" statehood had never existed' [12 *p. 203*]. Such was the force of the 'wind of change' that the Labour government of Harold Wilson* – which finally broke the thirteen years of Tory rule in 1964 – was faced with a 'settler revolt' in November 1965; the white-dominated government of Southern Rhodesia refused to succumb to 'African majority rule' and made its unilateral declaration of independence.

ECONOMICS AND THE END OF EMPIRE

Disenchantment with Colonial Economic Development

In Britain, the 1940s and the early 1950s had been a period of integrated, sterling-area economic development in which colonial economies were expected to produce commodities which would either earn or save dollars while, simultaneously, absorbing metropolitan manufactures. But from about 1953 there was a general disenchantment with the economic potentials of the colonies amongst influential circles in metropolitan Britain, especially as many development schemes ended in disaster. Most infamous was the East African Groundnuts Scheme: in 1949 the proposals of a working party sent to the Tanganyika mandate were accepted and the whole venture was closed down except for limited experimental work. The vast majority of the allotted budget was spent on clearing a mere 1.4 per cent of the planned total area of 3.2 million acres [7; 15, 2; 31]. '[T]his fiasco made the whole problem of removing obstacles to economic growth in Africa seem more intractable than ever' [31 *p. xlvii*]. Certainly such drastic state intervention in the colonies would not be tried again.

Colonial development clearly had not conjured up the much hoped for magical, 'multiplier effect' for the domestic economy. In the 1950s, Britain's share of world trade continued to decline accompanied by recurring sterling crises. The competitiveness of British manufacturers in terms of price and quality declined as producers such as West Germany and Japan recovered from the war. Despite preferential tariffs in favour of British goods in many colonies, British exporters even found the empire an increasingly tough market. British exports to colonial markets overall fell from 29 per cent to 23 per cent between 1953 and 1958; while, Britain's share of exports from the colonies correspondingly fell from 31 to 23 per cent in the same period [76 *p. 447*]. From as early as 1953, British economic policy was focused on the UK's own problems rather than those of the empire-sterling area as a whole. The root problem of British uncompetitiveness, it was reasoned, could not be solved by looking to the colonies to 'feather-bed' British manufactures. Instead, metropolitan trade policy became more and more concentrated on stimulating British exports to the dollar area to achieve a balance of trade [75].

Despite public pronouncements encouraging colonial investment, behind the scenes Treasury and Bank of England officials began to view free capital flows to the rest of the sterling area as a burden which starved domestic export industries of funds [75]. By the mid-1950s the Treasury was alarmed at the mounting costs of colonial development for the British Exchequer, not least because many British territories, such as the small Caribbean and Pacific islands, could generate only negligible resources in return for extensive grants-in-aid. As early as June 1952 one Treasury official commented that 'the whole conception of Commonwealth development as the solution to our difficulties is becoming something of a castle in the air' [*Doc. 8*]. The British private sector was also unwilling to pick up the colonial tab. During the 1950s colonial loans floated on the London money market proved consistently unpopular with City investors [15, 3 and 4; 63].

Those who still espoused the cause of the imperial economy found themselves increasingly marginalised. The 1954 Tory Party conference conclusively rejected imperial preference in favour of freer trade [9; 73], and, as the balance of payments of the sterling area improved, the Cabinet planned relaxations of import restrictions, despite the fact that the export trades of many colonies (notably the West Indies) would be hard hit by the loss of preferential access to the metropolitan market [63]. From 1955, moves were made to make sterling freely convertible [2; 75]. At the same time, new directions in British finance and industry by the later 1950s, and complementary metropolitan government policies, began to encourage domestic, European and North American rather than colonial transactions. Britain's powerful financial sector in the City of London now made demands for sterling convertibility and trade liberalisation to take advantage of the multilateral international economy. Colonial sterling balances became less important assets during the 1950s, and from 1957 the London banks began to turn away from the sterling area by entering the Euro-dollar market [2; 35; 65]. In 1957 the new Prime Minister, Harold Macmillan – who as Chancellor of the Exchequer between December 1955 and January 1957 had been 'fully exposed to a fiscal critique which was shot through with a new contempt for government spending in the colonies' [12 *p.* 207] – instituted an unprecedented cost-benefit review of the British Empire [15, 5]. The conclusions to this review, as Hopkins has argued, gave Macmillan what he needed; namely, an assurance that the empire could be dismantled without damaging British economic interests [65]. This bore fruit in Macmillan's decision to accelerate decolonisation in eastern and southern Africa after 1959 [11; 12].

The Attractions of Europe

Fearing exclusion from remunerative and expanding West European markets, Britain applied to join the European Economic Community (EEC) in 1961. This has been seen as a highly significant watershed in Britain's shift from imperial to regional economic interests. Formal moves towards European integration had been resisted under Churchill's premiership between 1951 and 1955. Britain was not completely 'Euro-sceptic' before the late 1950s: militarily, Britain had participated in West European defence through membership of NATO since 1949; economically, Britain was a member of the Organisation for European Economic Co-operation and the European Payments Union. None the less, up until the mid-1950s – at least – there was a general Conservative consensus to avoid more costly formal entwinements with continental Europe [63 *p. xxx*]. For Churchill, Britain's 'first object' was 'the unity and the consolidation of the British Commonwealth and what is left of the former British Empire' [182, 1 *p. 4*].

But with Churchill's retirement in 1955, the hand of the more pro-European Tories – most notably, Chancellor of the Exchequer Macmillan and the President of the Board of Trade, Peter Thorneycroft – was strengthened [63 *p. xxx*]. There were clear dangers that Britain might be excluded from the benefits of mainland Europe's economic dynamism, epitomised by the phoenix-like re-emergence of West German economic might [*Doc. 9*]. Moreover, in March 1957 the so-called 'Six' – West Germany, France, Italy, Belgium, the Netherlands, and Luxemburg – signed the Treaties of Rome, creating the EEC. Benefiting from high growth rates within its ranks, the EEC soon emerged as a powerful trading bloc.

Britain's response to European economic integration between 1956 and 1958 was the promotion of an alternative industrial Free Trade Area. This was an attempt to have the best of both worlds: Britain would be associated with the EEC while, simultaneously, maintaining its preferential trade arrangements with the Commonwealth and the colonies. The project failed because of disagreements with the EEC Six concerning the association of European colonial territories with the Free Trade Area which might have caused political problems in Africa and might have undermined the economic unity of Britain's empire and Commonwealth. Moreover, an industrial Free Trade Area was of little interest to European countries (particularly France) whose farmers wanted access to the British market for agricultural products.

Instead, in November 1959, the European Free Trade Association (EFTA) was formed which reduced tariffs among the 'Seven' – Austria, Denmark, Norway, Portugal, Sweden, Switzerland, and Britain – only [76; 82].

Yet, as decolonising territories increasingly realigned themselves to cheaper markets and more abundant sources of development finance, and British business became isolated from the international economic gains of the EEC, the Macmillan government became convinced of the need to make compromises. Entry into the EEC was now regarded as vital for the modernisation and expansion of British industry. As it turned out, the 1961 application was unsuccessful. It was vetoed by the French Premiere, Charles de Gaulle,* in 1963 on the grounds that Britain – with its close links to the Commonwealth and America – was still not 'European' enough [82]. The Gaullist 'snub', however, probably only increased the determination of Macmillan (and Wilson after him) to shed the last remnants of empire [11].

Britain's second EEC application in 1967 was again vetoed by de Gaulle who remained unconvinced by Wilson's pro-European rhetoric. But with the Commonwealth and sterling area outmoded, the Conservative government's 1971 White Paper declared that security, independence, economic strength and freer world trade were now best achieved through the EEC. British membership formally came into effect on 1 January 1973, principally because of a more congenial attitude in Paris under President Georges Pompidou on top of the Heath government's ready acceptance of the Treaty of Rome (even with its very limited guarantees for Commonwealth trade) [82]. The roots of this economic 'disengagement' from the empire-Commonwealth and the shift towards Europe can be traced back to the mid-1950s [*Doc. 9*].

GLOBAL STRATEGY AND THE END OF EMPIRE

The End of the 'Third Force'

Other important recalculations in Britain were diplomatic and military rather than economic. Between 1951 and 1956 the Conservative governments of Churchill and Eden had continued Attlee and Bevin's strategy to resist American pressures to redefine Britain's role as a regional, European power. The conviction that Britain should maintain a world role, independent of the United States, was exhibited by an imperial determination to remain ensconced in the Middle East, Africa and Asia. At the same time, Churchill and Eden instinctively distanced themselves from European integration and refused to become fully constrained by membership of NATO. The 'extra-European and extra-NATO dimensions to British interests' were epitomised by resources expended in the 1950s on colonial anti-insurgency wars in Malaya, Kenya, and Cyprus [12 *p. 202*] and a general commitment to limit rather than promote colonial constitutional change [62].

However, it is claimed, that Britain's attempt to play an autonomous, 'third force' world role came to an abrupt end in the Suez crisis of 1956 [12; 150]. American economic pressure forced the British – in concert with France and Israel – to quit their attempt to overthrow Egyptian President Nasser* and de-nationalise the Suez Canal Company (see Chapter 6). The failure of this attempt to reassert imperial power in the Middle East led to a *volte face* in British international strategy, involving a much closer alliance with the United States and the termination of traditional extra-European power politics. Macmillan, who succeeded Eden after the Suez débâcle, played the international game to American rules and within the confines of NATO. The key to Britain's position in the world now lay, in the light of Suez, in the maximisation of British influence within the anti-Soviet, Western Alliance. Thus, the elderly Macmillan developed a close relationship with the youthful American President, John F. Kennedy,* during the early 1960s which secured Britain's international status as America's most trusted and loyal ally in the Cold War. Necessarily, as the principal diplomatic priority in London became the maintenance of this 'special relationship', African and Asian commitments were sidelined in international agendas. Clearly, the resources Britain was prepared to expend on managing colonial change were severely reduced [11; 12].

Britain's moves toward Europe from the late 1950s were not solely motivated by the continent's economic prospects; a more pro-European policy also contained an important politico-strategic dimension. It was feared that the EEC might come to supplant Britain as America's chief ally. After all, the European bloc was a geopolitical entity approaching the dimensions of the two superpowers. If Britain remained outside such a structure its world influence – in both economic and political terms – would decline [55]. As one Foreign Office mandarin appreciated in 1960: 'the Commonwealth is not and will never be a source of power in absolute terms comparable with say the USA or possibly Western Europe' [55 *p. 160*].

The Nuclear Deterrent

Macmillan's new policy on the strategic front also called for a nuclear deterrent. In the 1957 Defence Review, Macmillan's administration secured a switch of resources from conventional to nuclear weaponry. It also foresaw the ending of conscription or 'National Service' in 1960 [*Doc. 10*]. Britain had fallen behind in the nuclear race after the war: in 1946 the Anglo-American partnership in nuclear technology ceased, and the Labour governments between 1945 and 1951 would not spare the resources to finance an independent programme. It was also believed that large-scale investment in nuclear weaponry was unnecessary given that the Soviet military threat was still conventional in both Europe and Asia [12; 64].

None the less, Labour was not completely anti-nuclear, and in 1947 a highly secret decision was taken by Attlee to make a British atomic bomb. This limited programme was inherited by Churchill in 1951. The elderly prime minister was increasingly pro-nuclear: atomic warheads seemed to be one means by which Britain could retain great power status and independence from the superpowers *without* colonial possessions [64]. As early as 1945, Churchill had appreciated that, 'the Atom bomb presaged a form of dominion in which the territorial size of the homeland counted for less, in which scientists (of which Britain had a great supply) were worth more than foreign exchange reserves (of which Britain had none at all), and which was based on "armies" of heavy metal rather than conscripted hordes' [13 *p. 196*]. Churchill's enthusiasm ensured that more public money was ploughed into Britain's nuclear programme: in October 1952 the first British atomic device was tested at Monte Bello in the Pacific [64]. In 1954, British defence policy moved further in the direction of the nuclear deterrent, with concurrent reductions in conventional forces. This had 'clear implications' for Britain's overseas military emplacements; for example, the new Anglo-Egyptian treaty looked forward to the evacuation of the Suez base by 1956. This huge military concentration was considered highly vulnerable in the event of nuclear warfare [63 *p. xxviii*]. By the mid-1950s, the Middle East was no longer central to British strategy [16].

Even so, by the time Macmillan became prime minister, British nuclear technology was still far inferior to that developed in the United States and the Soviet Union. The far larger investment secured in the 1957 Defence White Paper essentially wrote *finis* to large-scale colonial anti-insurgency campaigns. The decision to give up clamping-down on African nationalism after 1960 'arose logically from this strategic reorientation' [12 *p. 204*]. Yet, in this shift to a grand nuclear deterrence, Britain could not do without American assistance, particularly in the field of delivery systems. After 1958 then, Anglo-American atomic collaboration was re-established as a central feature of the 'special relationship' [64]. Close co-operation with the Americans culminated in the Nassau Agreement of December 1962 which provided American missiles for the British Polaris submarine fleet. 'The almost brazen confidence with which British officials went through the motions of successive decolonizations at Lancaster House undoubtedly bore some relationship to the prospect, and final achievement of this nuclear apotheosis' [11 *p. 180*].

PUBLIC OPINION AND THE END OF EMPIRE

There are also indications that something of an 'ethical revolution' took place within British society after 1945 which allowed many Britons to regard colonialism as morally bankrupt. The ending of the empire was one feature of a 'progressive mentality' epitomised by the creation of the welfare state in metropolitan Britain. Much of this was self-interest, of course: 'one reason' why colonies were ditched was to 'release resources' for 'domestic welfare spending' [12 *p. 209*]. Meanwhile many British youths, and their families, resented conscription into National Service especially if this meant being shot at in the distant and sweltering jungles of, say, Malaya.

But, whether for reasons grounded in morality or self-interest, by the late 1950s liberal journalists on *The Times*, The *Guardian*, The *Economist*, and The *Observer* ensured that London's quality press 'kept a close watch on the developing [decolonisation] scene and insisted that there should be sensitive hands on its tillers' [101 *p. 237*]. Official propaganda on the postwar radio continued to emphasise the virtues and unity of empire (particularly in the Queen's Christmas Speech to the empire and Commonwealth), while surprisingly vast efforts were made by successive British governments to justify colonial counter-insurgency campaigns through highlighting the supposedly illegitimate claims of Britain's opponents in these colonial wars [56; 70]. Yet, in mid-1959 publicisation of the beating to death of detained Mau Mau guerrillas at Hola Camp in Kenya and the Devlin Report's description of rioting Nyasaland as a 'police state', led to open criticism of colonial practice in parliament and the media [88; 101]. During the House of Commons debate on the Hola Camp incident the unpredictable young Tory MP, Enoch Powell, famously declared that, 'We cannot, we dare not, in Africa of all places, fall below our own highest standards in the acceptance of responsibility' [187, 2 *p. 513*].

Public opinion, in general, would appear to have supported Macmillan's decolonisation policies in the 1960s [101]. That coercion was not popular, especially when British lives were endangered, is confirmed by the Home Intelligence reports on India and domestic public opinion during the Second World War which found that, on the rare occasions when opinions were expressed, the British populace was 'on the side of conciliation and concession' [72 *p. 391*]. No doubt, ambivalence on colonial issues was also a result of the simple fact that, despite the odd balance-of-payments crisis, decolonisation coincided with an unprecedented 'golden age' of economic growth reinforced by a popular welfare state. Economic prosperity compensated for the loss of empire as a 'status good' [59]. None the less, progressive public opinion does seem to have had some influence on imperial policy by the later 1950s. Concern that the Conservatives might lose the support of younger, 'middle voters' in the general election of October 1959 was a major factor in convincing Macmillan that 'multiracialism' be abandoned in favour of 'one man, one vote' or 'majority rule' in eastern and southern Africa [74]. It would seem that little support from among the British populace could be relied upon for any last-ditch resurrection of empire, even in the improbable event that any government should have been so inclined.

THE CONTINUATION OF THE IMPERIAL VISION

The Commonwealth and the Preservation of Post-Colonial Influence

Alternatively, it could be argued, that British government, business and public views on empire did not fundamentally change in the course of the 1950s and 1960s. On the economic side of things, the value of empire markets was in decline from the early 1950s, but they were still worth keeping especially when juxtaposed against the uncertain commercial terrain of Western Europe [6; 55]. Indeed, empire and Europe were interdependent in British official and political minds. As a Cabinet minister, Reginald Maudling, explained in 1957: 'what strengthens the economy of the British Commonwealth must in the long run help to strengthen the economy of Europe, what strengthens the economy of Europe must help strengthen the economies of the British Commonwealth' [76 *p. 445*]. In May 1959, the influential Radcliffe Committee argued against dismantling or fundamentally modifying the sterling-area system. Indeed, there was a 'general harmony of interest between the UK economy and that of the rest of the Sterling Area' [*Doc. 11*]. It was expected (wrongly as it turned out) that, far from stagnating, 'the agricultural and mineral-based export economies' of the decolonising empire 'would experience rapid growth through rising commodity prices', and would, thus, provide valuable markets for British industry and profitable fields of investment for British finance in the future [19 *p. 172*]. Britain did apply to join the EEC in 1961, but, even at this stage, the Cabinet was not prepared to embrace the European market if this meant sacrificing the trade and investment preferences of the empire-Commonwealth [6 *p. 49*].

Likewise, Cabinet ministers remained lukewarm toward the prospects of closer political and strategic association with Europe. Interestingly, and clearly in the light of the Suez disaster, in 1957, Foreign Secretary Selwyn Lloyd put forward a grand scheme for closer alliance with the Western European Union, boldly declaring that, 'We should take our place where we now most belong, i.e. in Europe with our immediate neighbours'. In particular, this proposal looked forward to the development of a joint nuclear weapons programme since pooling resources with Europe was the only means of Britain remaining 'a first-class Power with full thermo-nuclear capacity' [63 *p. xxxi*]. But ministers did not agree and prioritised other interests: the preservation of Britain's independent nuclear capacity; the continuance of the 'special relationship' with America; and the maintenance of empire and Commonwealth defence links [63 *p. xxxi*; 182, 1 *Docs. 28–9*; 187, 2 *Docs. 68–9*]. Indeed, throughout its thirteen years of office from 1951, the Conservative Party's foreign policy consistently viewed empire, America and Europe as part of a 'Churchillian tripod' [5 *p. 234*]. Britain's leadership of the empire-Commonwealth, the 'special relationship' with the United States and 'closer association' with Europe were not necessarily three separate, mutually exclusive foreign policy options; rather, policy was geared to balancing the three elements in Britain's global outlook. In this sense, the moves toward Europe and the United States by the Macmillan government should not be interpreted as abandonment of the empire-Commonwealth [5; 55].

Indeed, for Darwin no real reassessment of Britain's place in the world took place after 1945. Through to the 1960s what occurred, instead, was the 'unpredictable erosion of position after position ... followed on each occasion by further efforts to hold together the remnants of world power and influence, by one means or another ... The pragmatic ingenious adaptation of British policy was geared, above all, to the preservation of British world power in increasingly adverse circumstances' [4 *p. 206*]. Independence for former British colonies was not perceived as representing an abrupt termination of metropolitan interests and involvement. Rather decolonisation was 'the translation of the colonial relationship into something more palatable in an age of Cold War and mass nationalism, a more flexible system of ties attuned to modern requirements' [55 p. 162]. In the course of 1957, for example, independence for both Malaya and Ghana was accompanied by the signing of economic and defence agreements which, it was hoped, would secure existing British interests in the successor states [50; 106].

The preservation of post-colonial 'influence', as opposed to the complete negation of empire, was a key tenet of British decolonisation strategy through the 1950s and 1960s. By meeting, rather than opposing, nationalist demands it was expected that developments in the colonies could be channeled along moderate lines and reserves of goodwill toward Britain could be built up. As the Commissioner-General in Southeast Asia, Malcolm MacDonald, told an audience of British businessmen in Singapore in August 1955, support for, rather than obstruction of, nationalist aspirations was: 'the best assurance that the process of change in Malaya shall continue to be peaceful and constitutional... causing the least possible upset to the economy and security of the country' [*Doc. 13*].

The creation of a new, multiracial Commonwealth – it was believed – was a central means of achieving these ends. The Commonwealth connection, it was hoped, would preserve British economic and strategic interests intact as it had in the 'white' Dominions since the middle of the nineteenth century [*Doc. 12*]. Despite persistent hopes for a status of less than full membership in the Commonwealth for smaller colonies to avoid 'dilution', the Conservatives, just like their Labour predecessors, appreciated that to deny full membership to newly independent Afro-Asian states would be politically damaging. As the Commonwealth Secretary, Lord Swinton, believed in 1954, the admission of former colonies to the Commonwealth would ensure that they stay 'within our own sphere of influence' and the 'existence of a Commonwealth composed of like-minded, independent and freely associating Members drawn from every continent, is a source of strength and prestige for the United Kingdom' [69 p. 257].

Once the small island of Cyprus had been admitted in 1961, the floodgates were opened to the expansion of the Commonwealth. It was regretted that the old intimacy of the white Commonwealth was lost, but in the Cold War this multiracial, multi-continental organisation allowed Britain, and the West in general, a continued influence in post-colonial states which the Soviets lacked [55; 69]. Such was the importance attached to the new multiracial character of the post-colonial club that Macmillan's government enthusiastically supported its expansion even at the expense of the departure of white-supremacist South Africa from the Commonwealth on racial grounds in 1961 [69].

The Commonwealth Consensus in British Politics

For many Conservative politicians the Commonwealth served as a surrogate empire which softened the blow of formal, imperial withdrawal. Indeed, an analysis of British political discourse on decolonisation exhibits little change of fundamental attitude towards empire. There was a remarkably cool, even indifferent, political reaction to imperial 'decline', largely because of the attractions of the Commonwealth ideal.

There were within the Conservative Party three overlapping 'diehard' groups which might have offered vigorous resistance to the acceleration of colonial self-government: the 'preferentialists' who opposed free trade in favour of close economic integration with the empire-Commonwealth during the 1950s; the so-called 'Suez group' of MPs who voted against the 1954 agreement under which British troops were to evacuate the Suez Canal base in 1956; and the white-settler lobby which in the early 1960s formed the Monday Club to oppose the rapid transfer of power to Africans in territories such as Kenya and Northern Rhodesia. But none of these groups were effective in altering the course of policy under the Churchill, Eden and Macmillan governments [6; 73]. Goldsworthy explains this by reference to the supposedly changing nature of the Conservative Party. From 1954 the older imperialist Tories were marginalised by their failure to economically unify the sterling area/Commonwealth as well as prevent the military withdrawal from Egypt and the later decolonisation of Cyprus. The final point of no return was reached following the 1959 election when a new breed of younger, more liberal, European-oriented Tory MPs entered parliament. The new Colonial Secretary, Iain Macleod*, appeared to accept the basic tenets of Labour's pragmatic decolonisation strategy and set about introducing black-majority rule in 'settler' Africa. Macmillan's remarkable 'wind of change' speech to the South African parliament in 1960 seemed to encapsulate the new anti-imperial orthodoxy [9] [*Doc. 26*].

Yet, on the other hand, Macmillan and his Cabinet colleagues continued to espouse traditional Tory values, particularly the concept of maintaining British global sway via the transformation of colonial rule into the Commonwealth connection. In this sense, Macmillan's policy was little different from that of Churchill and Eden before him. Indeed, this was a grand Tory tradition stretching back to the 1900s [14; 58]. The influence of the 'diehards' was limited because, in contradistinction to politicians in France, British Tory leaders found it relatively easy to argue that 'the winding up of colonial rule would not mean the end of predominant British influence' in vast swathes of the non-European world [6 *p. 33*]. 'Decolonization was the continuation of empire by other means' [58 *p. 42*]. Certainly for Macmillan in 1958 decolonisation was not a drastic change of course: 'though we no longer had authority, we still had great influence' [*Doc. 14*].

There were other reasons for stability within the Conservative Party: the strongly hierarchical nature of the party allowed for the prime minister and the Cabinet to get its way (even after the Suez crisis of 1956 there was no public enquiry) [6; 14; 58]. While the pragmatic role of business interests connected with Africa, the goal of multiracialism, and the preference for political solutions rather than the deployment of force in Africa, blurred the ideological divisions between liberal and imperialist tendencies [73]. But, above all, Macmillan and his cohorts relied on the idea of the Commonwealth as a cluster of former British territories, sharing the liberal values implanted in them by British rule, and which would 'remain part of a great British-centred world system' [6 *p. 36*] [*Doc. 12*]. The association of the monarchy with this imperial enterprise – the British crown became head of the Commonwealth – added further patriotic legitimacy. British public opinion, far from turning away from empire in moral disgust, was thus comfortably soothed by this new patriotic vision of Britain as *primus inter pares* in the multiracial Commonwealth [6; 58].

The Commonwealth ideal also appealed to significant sections in the Labour Party. There had always existed an 'anti-imperialist' tendency among Labour's ranks [6 *p. 25*]. When Labour returned to opposition in 1951 there was a breakdown in the remarkable consensus and bi-partisanship between the Labour and Tory parties on colonial issues which had characterised the Attlee years [9]. Anti-colonial factions within Labour such as Fenner Brockway's and Tony Benn's Movement for Colonial Freedom portrayed the Conservatives as backward-looking, blimpish racists [66]. In November 1959, for example, Benn sardonically and passionately observed in the Commons that those east and central African nationalists labelled 'extremists' were simply individuals 'who believe[d] that the Africans are entitled to the same full social, political and economic rights as the white man'; such 'aims and aspirations' were 'in common with everyone in this country and with the famous leaders of the last century who sought to bring equal political, economic and social rights to the working class in Britain' [187, 2 *p. 516*]. As Kahler claims: 'The strategy adopted by the Labour Party, one of unified and distanced opposition to colonialism, speeded decolonization' [14 *p. 362*].

Yet, there is little evidence that the Labour Party was united on colonial matters. While left-wing anti-colonial groups' undoubtedly influenced the course of parliamentary discussion of colonialism, it is doubtful whether they exerted influence on either Tory governments or Labour leaderships in the last years of empire. Rather, Labour's international outlook was still predicated that Britain should remain a world power, and that with the Commonwealth, Britain constituted a 'third force' in global affairs [6]. From 1956 Labour was committed to self-determination in eastern and southern Africa on the basis of 'one man, one vote'; Tory candidates were castigated during the 1959 election campaign for holding on to concepts of 'multiracialism' whereby the political privileges of white settlers would be maintained [10]. But this does not mean that the Labour front bench had given up on Britain still retaining considerable influence in the post-colonial world. As late as 1961, James Callaghan, Labour's spokesman on colonial affairs, reaffirmed the Party's commitment to shaping colonial developments in the interests of metropolitan Britain by the creation of a huge 'African Dominion' in east and central Africa [6 *p. 29*] [*Doc. 15*].

'East of Suez'

Labour's return to government after 1964 did witness the withdrawal from 'East of Suez' and another application to join the EEC. But the East of Suez decision came about not through a radical review but because of last minute decisions made in the light of the great sterling crisis of November 1967 which exposed the realities of Britain's international position. The East of Suez defence policy, ironically, gained greater pertinence under the Macmillan government in the wake of the Suez débâcle of 1956. It was an attempt to make the Indian Ocean a zone of British influence and military supremacy. Avoiding outright colonialism, this was to be achieved through strategically mobile forces backed up by bi-lateral agreements with semi-independent or recently independent countries, such as Oman or Malaysia, for base facilities and protection against radical subversion [13; 25]. 'However much British power and influence had been straitened elsewhere in the world, in the Indian Ocean, fringed by the vital oilfields of the Gulf, bordered by former colonial territories in Africa, South and South East Asia, and traversed by vital air and sea routes to Australia and New Zealand, Britain was to remain a great power' [5 *p. 290*].

The emphasis on Britain's role in the Indian Ocean continued into Wilson's regime. Indeed, in New Delhi in June 1965 Wilson announced that 'Britain's frontiers are on the Himalayas' [5 *p. 291*], and the Wilson government continued a vast military commitment in Southeast Asia during the undeclared war, or 'Confrontation', to defend Malaysia from Indonesian aggrandisement. Up until the end of 1967, Wilson persistently resisted pressures to devalue the pound or cut British military commitments in the Middle East and Southeast Asia. But, in the aftermath of the currency crisis, the Labour government was forced to slash public expenditure and naturally targeted the 'fag-end of empire' [25; 57; 81] [*Doc. 16*]. The financial débâcle of 1967 finally presaged the end of the sterling area in 1972 [2; 68].

Labour's 'Great Britain' policy between 1964 and 1968 presents a 'curious paradox' which Darwin emphasises: 'at the time when colonial rule was being drawn to a close by a Conservative government in later 1950s and early 1960s, and the old party of empire was moving towards an application to the EEC, the Labour party took up more and more emphatically the mantle of the Commonwealth' [6 *p. 27*]. The EEC was often regarded by left-wing politicians as an inward-looking, 'rich man's club' which would 'increase food prices, bring greater unemployment (due to continental competition) and end Labour's ability to pursue socialist policies at home' [82 *p. 111*]. In contrast, 'the Commonwealth had become the crucial instrument whereby British influence could promote more or less utopian visions of East-West amity and North-South harmony' [6 *p. 27*]. For example, Wilson's June 1965 peace initiative on Vietnam was made through the Commonwealth as a 'third force' (being neither American nor communist) [81]. Both Socialist and Tory Britains, then, were clearly not Little Englands.

'NEO-COLONIALISM'

The Continuation of Colonial Economic Dependency

Both Labour and Conservative emphases on the Commonwealth as a means of preserving Britain's extra-European interests might point to a strategy of 'neo-colonialism'. On this Marxist argument, disengagement from empire did not occur during the 1950s and 1960s. Rather, the continuity of large-scale British investments and markets in the former empire suggests that imperialism survived decolonisation intact. It could be argued that Western capitalism had evolved to such a point that colonial rule became redundant. Constitutional progress in the colonial empire did not damage Britain's economic interests, and indeed may even have enhanced them. Imperial and colonial governments, serving the interests of metropolitan capitalism, transferred power to 'moderates' to pre-empt real economic and social change in the periphery. Settlements were reached with compliant nationalists which successfully preserved 'for the mother country as many of the advantages as possible' while, at the same time, preventing 'social revolutions directed to real independence for the former colonies' [71 p. 164]. Power was prematurely transferred to 'collaborators' who would keep their economies capitalist and export-orientated, and who could maintain strong magisterial functions and labour discipline. Hence, colonial cultural, strategic, and, above all, economic dependence on the imperial metropolis would continue after independence.

The classic case study is by Wasserman on early-1960s Kenya. The modernised and 'liberal' expatriate plantation and commercial sectors in Kenya outmanoeuvred the 'conservative', die-hard settlers. The former's decolonisation strategy was to forge an alliance with the African bourgeoisie to preserve the colonial open economy intact. Via close ties with the British Conservative Party, access to government policy-makers in both metropole and periphery, and financial and administrative backing for moderate nationalist groups, the business interests represented by Michael Blundell's* New Kenya Group managed decolonisation [79]. Certainly, Kenya's dependence on British capital was understood by its first Prime Minister, Jomo Kenyatta,* when he went out of his way to assure expatriate business leaders that their investments would be safe under 'African Socialism' [Doc. 17].

Problems with Neo-Colonialism

As with any grand theory of imperialism, a number of pitfalls have been identified with the 'neo-colonialism' or 'dependency' approach. It suggests a degree of control on the part of the imperial power which is probably unrealistic; it overestimates 'the freedom of manoeuvre' which both British governments and British firms 'enjoyed, as well as the extent to which colonial nationalism ... could be bought off and accommodated' [5 p. 23]. Nationalist politicians were hardly the lackeys of metropolitan capital, and the British could not guarantee that figures, such as Kenyatta, would uphold their economic interests after independence.

It also seems unlikely that British businesses and governments could anticipate the favourable outcomes of decolonisation. In the case of Unilever, the end of formal empire certainly did not curtail the activities of the Anglo-Dutch multinational enterprise and often provided new opportunities. But the origins of Unilever's local production in west Africa were a result of reactions to new developments in the

1950s – notably the need to evade the restrictions of tariff barriers introduced by self-governing regimes. Unilever executives did not create or seek to influence these events. Moreover, the transition from empire to Commonwealth was not an inconsequential or maximising process. Decolonisation ended the political security enjoyed by Unilever, and from now on it was evident that, 'direct investment in most lesser developed countries, must be treated as risk capital. This ... was the crux of the international revolution labelled decolonization' [60 *p. 601*].

Simply because the 'economic links between the one-time metropolises and the new states ... remained close after independence' does not necessarily mean that 'such results were expected and that these expectations encouraged officials and capitalists to look forward to decolonisation without fear' [61 *p. 6*]. In Southeast Asia, the British were successful in crushing communism and transferring power to a moderate Malayan government in the 1950s which did not fundamentally challenge British dominance of the economy. This has been seen as a classic example of neo-colonialism. However, the British agency houses in Malaya were far from optimistic about the postcolonial future and feared that the Alliance government would soon disintegrate or be forced to take a more radical economic course [80].

There is also an inherent danger of assuming that government and business acted in unison during the decolonisation process. In the cases of Malaya, the Gold Coast, Kenya, Nigeria and Egypt businesses were not only divided among themselves, but often disagreed fundamentally with British official strategies for political and economic development. As a result, expatriate enterprises and business associations appear to have had little determining influence on government policy [77; 78; 80].

The British Empire after 1945 continued to be made up of a hotchpotch of dependencies at varied levels of economic sophistication. Darwin finds it difficult to believe that 'in all, or even many of these very different cases, British policy-makers were invariably preoccupied with smoothing the path for [British firms] by striking prompt bargains with suitably "moderate" nationalists' [6 *p. 53*]. 'In their efforts to "manage" colonial nationalism, the British had many other aims in mind besides promoting the interests of international capital' [6 *p. 53*]. In Cyprus, for example, the Cabinet's overriding concern in the 1950s was to protect treasured strategic, not economic, interests. The huge military build up on the Mediterranean island during the 1950s – including the completion of the largest British air base overseas, RAF Akrotiri, in 1957 – made Cyprus vital to British Cold War strategy. As a result, when the British conceded political independence to Cyprus in 1960, this was conditional upon the continued British military presence in a number of 'Sovereign Base Areas' [67]. In other words, decolonisation served a variety of British diplomatic, military and economic interests.

Moreover, the hope that the transition from empire to Commonwealth would preserve and expand Britain's overseas trade and investment proved fantasy. 'Optimistic forecasts' about the growth potential of the Commonwealth economies proved 'badly wrong' as the terms of trade of developing countries declined by some 16 per cent between 1955 and 1965, making them decidedly 'less valuable' as markets and fields of investment [19 *p. 172*]. Far from an intensification of the links between metropole and colony, there was a loosening of economic ties between Britain and its 'client states' in the late colonial and, especially, in the post-colonial era. The 1960s and 1970s witnessed a significant reorientation of trading and investment patterns as both Britain and its major Commonwealth commercial partners looked to America, Europe and Japan for economic salvation [6 *p. 50*]. In this sense, the real financial beneficiaries of decolonisation were not established British firms but expanding American, German and Japanese transnationals.

Commonwealth Immigration

Britain's indirect influence on former colonial territories was also eroded by restrictions placed on Commonwealth immigration into the 'motherland'. The British Nationality Act of 1948 had confirmed the status of 'Commonwealth citizen' with the same rights as a British subject. In principle this appeared to guarantee to all empire and Commonwealth subjects the right of abode in the United Kingdom.

But the right of free entry became increasingly difficult for Conservative governments to defend as immigration, particularly from the Caribbean and South Asia, expanded dramatically in the 1950s. The racist response of the British electorate to mass, non-white immigration into Britain eventually culminated in the 1962 Commonwealth Immigration Act which limited the free flow of immigrants. Labour leader Hugh Gaitskell protested that this risked the end of the Commonwealth as a meaningful entity, but, realising that anti-racism lost votes, Labour's return to office in 1964 under Harold Wilson witnessed intensified controls on immigration [187; 2 *pp. 76–7*]. Ironically, Commonwealth immigration policy 'was the only [decolonisation] issue on which public opinion seems to have engaged with any intensity' [72 *p. 380*]. It was also a major factor in *reducing* the possibility of British world influence through the post-colonial relationship.

AFTERWORD: THE EMBARRASSING REMNANTS

By the end of the 1960s the 'wind of change' had blown through most of Britain's major colonies. Overseas territories were such an international embarrassment that, to Britain's ultimate relief, even the white settlers of Southern Rhodesia eventually yielded to black-majority rule as Zimbabwe emerged in 1980. (This followed an intense guerrilla war and internationally imposed – although, in practice, rather ineffectual – economic sanctions against the recalcitrant regime of Ian Smith) [5; 12].

Yet, Britain has retained a scattering of colonial territories. Some of these contain such small populations – such as Pitcairn, Tristan da Cunha, St Helena, Ascension, Bermuda and the 'Associated States' in the West Indies – that independence would be economically unviable. None the less, some very small, 'micro-states', particularly in the Pacific Ocean, were hustled into independence. Other territories continue to be retained because of 'wider international considerations' [5 *p. 308*]. The claims of Argentina to the Falklands Islands and Spain to Gibraltar have negated against the transfer of sovereignty in these colonies of limited economic or strategic value. In the case of the Falklands, the determination of parliamentary and public opinion in Britain that a 'British' population should not fall under the control of an Argentinian military government culminated in the Anglo-Argentinian war of 1982 in which the deaths of two thousand persons – on both sides – exceeded the total population of the islands. As Darwin perceptively comments, 'had more British colonies been threatened by annexationist neighbours, the whole history of Britain's retreat from empire might have been very different – more painful and much more controversial' [5 *p. 314*].

In 1997, however, Britain returned the colony of Hong Kong to China. This involved delivering a territory to a communist regime which both the colonial people and Britain reviled. Up to the 1980s the British had resisted any constitutional change in Hong Kong, principally fearing adverse reactions on the Chinese mainland. Full independence was fraught with danger since it might have provoked a Chinese invasion. Moreover, both China and Britain had an interest in maintaining the *status quo* as Hong Kong emerged as a major financial centre, and the principal link between the Chinese economy and the capitalist world [5; 53]. However, in 1984, with Britain's lease from China of the New Territories – which made up the majority of the colony – nearing expiry, the Anglo-Chinese Agreement on the Future of Hong Kong was signed. Hong Kong would revert to China in 1997 but the existing economic and social structures would remain for at least fifty years and, generally, the former colony would enjoy a high degree of autonomy from Beijing. In the transitional period between 1984 and 1997, Britain attempted to prepare for an 'honourable exit' from Hong Kong. But plans for greater democratisation came up against the intransigent Chinese who pledged to overturn even the limited liberalisations of the last years of British rule. Britain's withdrawal was also marred by its refusal to grant British passports to all but a minority of Hong Kong's population [68].

PART THREE: NATIONALISM AND DECOLONISATION

4 CHANGING COLONIAL SOCIETIES

THE REVOLTING PERIPHERY

In May 1960 the former British Prime Minister, Clement Attlee, opined in a lecture at Oxford that, 'There have been many great Empires in the history of the world that have risen, flourished for a time, and then fallen. ... There is only one Empire where, without external pressure or weariness at the burden of ruling, the ruling people has voluntarily surrendered its hegemony over subject peoples and has given them their freedom. ... This unique example is the British Empire' (*Empire Into Commonwealth*, 1961, *p. 1*). Here was a classic statement of the liberal Commonwealth tradition or imperial mission; decolonisation as the honourable fruition of British deliberation and benevolence. However, it could be argued, that British policy simply reacted to events in the colonial 'periphery'; decolonisation was determined not by British officials and politicians but by the colonial peoples themselves in the guise of nationalist movements. The British faced intense violence in territories such as Malaya, Kenya and Cyprus and, virtually everywhere, colonial rule crumbled far quicker and decolonised states took forms unforeseen by British planners [101].

Contemporary studies of decolonisation in action, such as Thomas Hodgkin's classic work *Nationalism in Tropical Africa* (1956), stressed the growth of colonial protest in multifarious forms. From the 1960s, however, Western liberals were reluctant to legitimise the authoritarian rulers of successor states, while ethnic 'sub-nationalisms', tragic civil wars, and class divisions strained confidence in Third-World nationhood [115]. British historians of decolonisation concentrated instead on metropolitan interpretations based upon newly opened documents drawn from the Public Record Office in London. It is suggested that there is an inherent bias in these government sources which down-play 'the case for initiatives and move-ments in the colonies themselves' [97 *p. 17*].

There have, however, been attempts to place anti-colonial nation-alism at the centre of decolonisation analysis. Radical anti-colonial-ism across the empire in the 1940s and 1950s, it is claimed, scuppered Colonial Office and Cabinet agendas for gradual devolution [89; 101; 114]. Studies of the tropical empire after 1945 find echoes in the bat-tles fought out in Indian historiography. The so-called 'Cambridge school' has down-graded the role of popular initiatives in India, emphasising instead the uneven development of nationalism, competi-tion between provincial elites, and controlled British constitution making [86; 91; 110]. But others have stressed the growth of a broad-based national movement – particularly amongst the Indian peasantry – which forced the British into successive constitutional retreats between 1917 and 1947 [101; 109].

THE BEGINNINGS OF COLONIAL NATIONALISM

Colonial nationalism did not suddenly emerge at the end of the Second World War. Colonial societies experienced a number of eco-nomic, sociocultural and political changes in the course of the nine-teenth and twentieth centuries which laid the basis for mass nationalisms after 1945. In seeking the origins of colonial nationalism, some have emphasised a tradition of resistance and rebellion stretching back to the imposition of colonial rule [85; 103]. On the other hand, it has been argued that colonial polities were essentially characterised by 'collaboration' with established local elites. When the pool of suit-able collaborators evaporated in the second half of the twentieth cen-tury, colonial rule came to its logical end [8; 90; 107]. An alternative approach suggests that the real key to the maintenance of colonial authority was the 'assuagement' of the 'rich' peasantry. Britain's growing failure to assuage its colonial subjects' demands, rather than a lack of collaborators, led to the empire's systematic demise from Asia to Africa [101].

Whichever vision of interaction between colonial subject and imperial master is correct, it remains clear that the maintenance of colonial control was becoming more problematic in the course of the twenti-eth century. Colonial rule was not a static entity, but brought about a number of subtle changes which led ultimately to its downfall. As Benedict Anderson has argued the 'nation' in many colonial societies was not a 'natural' phenomenon, but was an 'imagined community' which had to be created. The growth of education, communications, transport and legal systems, which all resulted from the spread of colonial rule and the concomitant development of capitalist modes of production, were vital elements in the 'imagining' of national communities in much of the colonial world [83]. Potentially subversive philosophies were also introduced by the Christian missionaries, particularly in Africa [10]. Meanwhile, economic changes, in the form of urbanisation and the growth of colonial export industries, assisted the process of ethnic and national solidarity and threw up new articulate middle classes [10].

Indeed, Asia and Africa's increased integration into the international economy exposed underlying tensions in many colonial societies. This was particularly the case during the Great Depression of the 1930s. From 1929 onwards there was a severely reduced demand, and hence a sharp fall in prices, for primary products [52; 96]. The political fall-out from economic distress was most marked in India. The Indian National Congress, under the spiritual leadership of M. K. Gandhi, directed a number of Civil Disobedience campaigns which encompassed much of the subcontinent during the early 1930s. Congress activists achieved a mass base of support by tapping into the grievances of peasants, workers and industrialists, and forced the British to accelerate political reform throughout India [101; 109].

Problems of colonial control were further exacerbated by the Second World War. Declining living standards and restrictions on political activities often accompanied the war effort [6; 96; 109]. Meanwhile, the occupation of much of Asia and the Pacific by a non-European power, Japan, was a signpost for the end of empire. In Southeast Asia, British possessions were under Japanese occupation by 1942. In Burma and Malaya, the Japanese encouraged nationalists either directly through the establishment of puppet regimes and movements or indirectly through provoking resistance forces [111]. Wartime experiences also expanded the international consciousness of Africans, many of whom served in the armed forces overseas [*Docs. 18 & 19*]. The 'Quit India' campaign of 1942 encapsulated imperial wartime strains. Frustrated at the lack of progress toward independence, Congress demanded in August 1942 an immediate end to British rule and began another all-India campaign of non-co-operation. The movement was suppressed by the *Raj*. But the Indian historian, Sarkar, concludes that the British ultimately came to realise the wisdom of a negotiated transfer of power following the 'Quit India' campaign [109].

Yet, while in South Asia nationalist movements stretched back to the beginning of the century, colonial protest movements in Africa,

Malaysia, the Pacific and the Caribbean were limited in their appeal, scope and effectiveness before 1945 [101]. African, Southeast Asian or West Indian nationalism, as it existed before the 1940s, was confined to an urban elite which did not penetrate the rural hinterlands. The elite nationalists themselves were far from united and coherent groups: the aims of African intellectuals, for example, varied from ethnic solidarity to territorial nationalism to 'Pan-Africanism'. In such an environment, the British were still free to consolidate their alliances with the traditional rulers in the colonial countryside, and contain embryonic anti-colonial movements [10; 19]. It was the more immediate changes of the later 1940s and early 1950s which allowed for the mobilisation of mass discontent throughout most of the empire.

THE GROWTH OF MASS NATIONALISMS AFTER 1945

Economic Problems in Africa

In Africa economic conditions remained poor after the war. This was manifest in the numerous strikes which engulfed Africa in the mid- to late-1940s, co-ordinated by new trade unions [114 *p. 13*]. In 1945, a strike of railway and government workers in Nigeria involved some 30,000 people in the capital Lagos alone, protesting at low wages and high prices and thus illustrating how 'wartime hardships had increased class-conscious[ness]' among Africans. The Nigerian strikes followed upon the formation of the National Council of Nigeria and the Cameroons (NCNC) in 1944 under the leadership of Nnamdi Azikiwe* ('Zik'). The ultimate aim of Zik's movement was self-government for Nigeria [10 *p. 76*]. In 1949, violent confrontation with the colonial state broke out at the Enugu coalfields, resulting in the deaths of twenty-one striking miners and the spread of unrest throughout eastern Nigeria [78]. For Nigeria as a whole, it is estimated that between 1945 and 1950 over 100,000 man-days were lost to strike action [96]. East Africa was also ablaze with radical union activity: in January 1947 the dockers of Mombasa (Kenya) led a general strike which threatened to envelop the overcrowded capital, Nairobi. Further south, in Dar es Salaam (Tanganyika), another docker-led protest mushroomed into a territory-wide strike as it engulfed the sisal plantations, lead mines and the Groundnut Scheme [98; 113; 114]. In Southern Rhodesia, meanwhile, a general strike of African workers encompassed Bulawayo, Salisbury and other towns during 1948 [84].

Probably 'the most important protest' in postwar British Africa took place in February 1948 in the Gold Coast [114 *p. 13].* The capital of this west-African 'model' colony, Accra, encapsulated urban Africa's post-war economic and social problems. Housing conditions were atrocious. Demobbed soldiers exacerbated the already serious unemployment situation. Moreover, vastly inflated retail prices prevailed for imported consumer goods thanks largely to import controls to conserve desperately needed dollars for the sterling area. A boycott of European import stores began in January 1948, but prices remained high. On 28 February a protest march of ex-servicemen got out of control and was fired on by police. Two died. There followed three days of rioting which extended from Accra inland to Kumasi. The boycotts and riots appear to have been spontaneous protests. But, believing they were the first stage in an attempted communist coup, Governor Creasy declared a 'state of emergency' and detained six leaders of the United Gold Coast Convention (UGCC), including the movement's new charismatic, socialist General-Secretary, Kwame Nkrumah [93; 105; 106; 114] [*Doc. 19].*

The 'Second Colonial Occupation' in Africa

Disaffection in colonial Africa was rural as well as urban. Peasant producers became disaffected with governments who paid artificially low prices for their crops via state-run Commodity Marketing Boards (which were introduced during the war). Moreover, the 'second colonial occupation' precipitated an upsurge of protest in rural Africa [37; 98; 100; 101; 113; 114]. After 1945, demands for colonial economic development were intensified. But there were fatal flaws in the new imperial strategy of crashing into development because it led to an unprecedented intrusion into the affairs of colonial subjects [8]; not only was there a great increase in the number of British officials but they also brought with them a set of deeply resented dictates designed to improve the efficiency of peasant agriculture [101]. A principal concern was the danger of soil erosion leading to mass malnutrition. Hence, agricultural officers intervened in local peasant practice. In east and central Africa, for example, the construction of terraces and the introduction of new famine relief crops was encouraged. But changes in agricultural methods were frequently unpopular with Africans. As a result, stiff penalties and compulsory labour were employed to enforce agricultural rules [114] [Doc. 20]. In Kenya, Kikuyu peasant families were required to devote two mornings per week to the construction of terraces as part of the communal labour scheme. Such well-meaning, long-term policies only produced disaffection and there were rural disturbances in 1947. Discontent was multiplied by mass expulsions of 'squatters' and urban unemployment, housing shortages and destitution. Control of local politics increasingly passed from the moderates to the militants in the violent underground movement known as the Mau Mau. Secret oathing ceremonies bound peasants to resistance and led to armed rebellion by the end of 1952 [113; 114] [*Doc. 18*]. Contrary to British claims at the time, there is no evidence that the Kikuyu leader, Jomo Kenyatta, was ever associated with the Mau Mau. But the sheer cost of suppressing the rebellion finally marginalised the reactionary white settler interests, and allowed 'moderate' Africans, like Kenyatta, to negotiate independence with Macmillan's Conservative government in the early 1960s. '[O]nce the peasantry was roused', Throup tells us, 'the days were numbered for colonial rule' [113 *p. 248*].

Expanding political consciousness in east Africa was given a further fillip by suspicion of those white settlers who advocated economic development through a 'closer union' of Kenya, Uganda and Tanganyika. The proposed East African Federation would necessarily fall under the control of the European minority [10 *p. 77*]. Black Africans only had to look to central Africa to appreciate what this would mean: Southern Rhodesia had been given full self-government in 1923 but only whites could exercise full political and civil rights. As in neighbouring South Africa, black Africans were subject to racist colour-bars and pass laws while the best land was reserved for European agriculture and industry. The administration and the police were also firmly in the hands of European officers, and in 1948 only 258 Africans were registered in an electorate of 47,000 [10 *p. 81*].

Peasant anger was intensifed by the growing interventionism of the settler regime in Southern Rhodesia. Evictions of 'squatters' and their cattle – on a far larger scale than even Kenya – were carried out to accommodate the large postwar, 'second colonial invasion' of immigrant settlers [10] [*Doc. 20*]. At the same time, rigorous conservation measures were enforced, compulsory labour employed, and systems of land tenure revised, to meet ecological problems. These measures were widely resented by peasant farmers in the African reserves who formed the natural constituency of the nationalist movements which emerged by the later 1950s and were led by the disenfranchised African intelligentsia. Peasant grievances, particularly concerning the loss of tribal lands and fired by memories of primary resistance to the colonialists at the turn of the century, fed into the guerrilla war against the white regime during the 1970s [84; 104]. In Northern Rhodesia and Nyasaland – where compulsory agricultural rules had also been implemented – moves towards a fully self-governing Central African Federation (with Southern Rhodesia) after 1953 only served to intensify peasant, worker and intelligentsia fears of white domination. Northern Rhodesia and Nyasaland had also experienced a postwar influx of white settlers from Britain and South Africa [10; 29] [*Doc. 20*]. The 'second colonial occupation' swooped upon rural west Africa too (although devoid of the mass white settler invasions): in the Gold Coast, many cocoa trees were infected with swollen shoot disease which threatened this huge dollar-earning export industry. The colonial government's agricultural technicians demanded the felling of diseased trees. This was resisted by the African farmers since even infested trees continued to provide a harvest of marketable cocoa pods for several years. In December 1946, the colonial government resorted to a provocative compulsory cutting-out campaign, without solving the issue of compensation and replanting grants until after the 1948 riots [105; 106; 114] [*Doc. 19*]. The strength of peasant resistance to well-meaning rural reforms, as well as urban rioting in protest at declining living standards, may have caught many nationalist politicians by surprise: the anti-colonial revolution, as in India before the war, was 'subaltern' in character, co-ordinated, rather than instigated, by the nationalist elite [100; 101; 109].

The Growth of Political Parties and the Acceleration of Constitutional Change in Africa

Poor economic and social conditions, and the increasing encroachments of the 'second colonial occupation', only served to exacerbate political frustrations. In much of colonial Africa after 1945 living standards were slowly recovering from the deprivations of the Depression and war years. But these limited improvements failed to keep up with African aspirations which had been encouraged by British promises of a 'New Deal' after the war [96]. In particular, the lack of access to political power was highlighted despite British talk of constitutional change: the examples of Indian, Ceylonese and Burmese independence did not go unnoticed in Africa [*Doc. 19*]. Nationalist political parties emerged as the best means to articulate these postwar African grievances. 'Nationalist politics ... condemned the colonial state as an essentially transitory phenomenon unable to make the transition to full modernization. But nationalist organisations claimed to be more than just modern political machines intent on wresting control of state power. The politics of nationalism, infused with traditional symbolism and idiom, fiercely defended indigenous society against alien encroachment' [19 *p. 105*].

'African nationalists ... were ... able to bind rural discontent over the prices they received and over government intervention, to urban discontent at inflation and appalling housing conditions and growing unemployment' [114 *p. 16*]. The solution seemed logical: political empowerment for Africans and the termination of colonial rule. For example, Nkrumah's Convention Peoples' Party (CPP) in the Gold Coast, formed in 1949 and much more radical than the merchants and lawyers in the UGCC, was able to count on the support of mass organisations such as the trade unions in the towns and the farmers' associations in the villages which guaranteed the requisite support for non-co-operation campaigns and election victories. The CPP was thus able to create a genuinely populist alliance of urban and rural, elite-intellectual and mass; exactly the type of alliance which had eluded the Gold Coast intelligentsia before the war. Gold Coast nationalism had thus expanded from the preserve of a small urban-based, western-educated elite to a truly populist phenomenon. Moreover, Nkrumah's organisation broke the hold of the traditional chiefs – the collaborative agents of British 'indirect rule'– on mass political allegiances [93; 105].

The element of political change unleashed by the Labour government in London now spiralled beyond British control. The British hoped, of course, to foster elected local councils and so divert nationalist attention away from the centre. But the African Local Self-Government Circular Despatch of 1947 had the opposite effect: 'territories which had been political deserts now seemed to pullulate with political parties that were the darlings of the masses, the tribunes of the people and the voice of the people' [8 *p. 148*]. Attempts to develop moderate, non-communist trade unions – as part of Labour's progressive social welfare package for the empire – also backfired on British officials since nationalist leaders frequently came to employ the unions as organs of anti-colonial protest [101].

Pressures from within Africa, particularly after 1948, considerably modified the slow and moderate path to decolonisation envisaged by planners within the Colonial Office [93; 101; 114]. The Gold Coast serves as the classic example. In May 1947 a conference of African governors and Colonial Office officials had concluded that even for the Gold Coast – the most politically advanced territory in Africa – 'internal self-government is unlikely to be achieved in much less than a generation ...' [106 *p. xlv*]. However, in the aftermath of the 1948 riots, the Coussey Committee of enquiry recommended an element of internal self-government. Much greater emphasis, therefore, was being placed on political and constitutional development at the centre rather than in the locality as previously [106].

Even so, it was expected that the political successors to the British colonial bureaucrats would be the traditional band of collaborating chiefs and moderate middle-class intellectuals, hence excluding the demagogic young firebrands in the CPP. Yet, in the 1951 elections, the CPP, following a Gandhian-style campaign of non-co-operation in January 1950 known as 'Positive Action', swept the board. Nkrumah was released from prison and became the Leader of Government Business (and later prime minister). There followed a period of power-sharing ('dyarchy') between African ministers and colonial officials in which the British hoped to contain nationalism. However, after having proved its national majority in two further elections (1954 and 1956), the CPP led the colonial Gold Coast to independence as Ghana in March 1957. Nkrumah became independent Ghana's first prime minister [105; 106]. Britain's other principal west African colonies, Nigeria and Sierra Leone, followed closely behind in 1960 and 1961 respectively.

But, in east and central Africa the British still hoped in the late 1950s for a rather more gradual timetable for independence. Because of the presence of significant Indian, Arab and European communities, British planners looked forward to the development of 'multiracial' constitutions based on 'partnerships' between African majorities and European and Asian minorities. '[T]he long-established mechanics of British colonial polities – with their executive and legislative councils, and delicate balances struck between nominated officials and elected unofficials, the latter often on communal "rolls" – provided an almost unlimited prospect for fine gradations in the devolution of power leading to local (but not necessarily majority) self-government. ... [T]he constitutional time-tables in "settler" Africa trailed off as far as the eye could see' [13 *p. 263*]. But by 1959 it became clear – with unworkable multiracial constitutions in east Africa and riots and emergencies in Nyasaland and the two Rhodesias – that the 'partnership' or 'multiracialism' concept was bankrupt. Africans clearly wanted 'majority rule' [84; 88; 101]. The passing of Kenya, Tanganyika and Uganda into independence and the dismantling of the Central African Federation, it is suggested, were primarily dictated by the Macmillan government's concern to avert large-scale insurrections. 'African nationalism proved to be no respector of the distinction between British West and British East and Central Africa' [101 *pp. 231–2*].

The 'Second Colonial Occupation' in Southeast Asia

The cumulative political effects of economic distress and the 'second colonial occupation' were not confined to Africa alone. The British return to Malaya – after the Japanese occupation – was muddied by inflation, food shortages, and low wages. The Malayan Communist Party (MCP) led strikes of ethnic Chinese and Indian labourers on the rubber plantations and in the tin mines which seriously threatened the position of British capitalism in the empire's prime dollar-earning territory. Industrial unrest blended with a general sense of crisis and anxiety in rural areas and on the forest frontier [94; 112]. In addition, the Malay population was mobilised on an all-Malaya scale for the first time in protest at Britain's radical Malayan Union plan which threatened the sovereignty of the sultans and, hence, Malay political supremacy. Faced by a possible loss of control, the British substituted the Union for Federation in February 1948.

But this only served to further marginalise the large Chinese community, and did not solve the problem of communist-co-ordinated labour unrest. The murder of three British planters by MCP militants in June 1948 led to the declaration of the Emergency, and the beginnings of Britain's most protracted and intense war of decolonisation which finally ended in 1960, three years after Malayan independence [50; 112].

The Emergencies

Britain's resort to colonial war in Malaya is, perhaps, indicative of a postwar 'crisis of empire' induced by the growth of radical, populist anti-colonial nationalism. According to Frank Füredi, a mass politicisation took place across the British Empire from the Solomon Islands in the Pacific to British Guiana on the South American mainland. If the British were to preserve their economic and strategic interests they had to act. In some cases – e.g. in the Gold Coast and in Jamaica – this was a relatively peaceful and tension-free process; nationalist leaders were co-opted into colonial government and nationalism was managed through political and constitutional means. In other cases, however, there was far less room for manoeuvre and the British were forced to deal with radical nationalism through military means. They relied on the tactic of declaring 'emergencies' (colonial wars).

Emergencies were stop-gap measures which allowed the British to buy time and bolster alternative moderate nationalists who would not substantially threaten imperial interests. At the same time, the British expended considerable effort on propaganda campaigns which presented their opponents in colonial wars – for example, ethnic Chinese communists in Malaya and Mau Mau forest fighters in Kenya – as unrepresentative nationalists lacking in popular legitimacy. These military interventions allowed for the 'recasting of Third World nationalism'. But, in the first instance, it was anti-colonial pressure, as opposed to changing metropolitan priorities, which dictated decolonisation strategies. Historians who deny this, says Füredi, are subconsciously seeking to vindicate colonial rule [89].

The role of nationalism – whether radical or moderate – in dictating events was appreciated by the British Official Committee on Commonwealth Membership of 1954. It informed Churchill's Cabinet that decolonisation 'cannot now be halted or reversed ... the pace of constitutional change will be determined by the strength of nationalist feeling and the development of political consciousness within the territory concerned' [*Doc. 21*]. Such an admission would seem to bear out the 'peripheral theory' or 'excentric approach' pioneered by Ronald Robinson: 'the inversion of collaboration into non-cooperation largely determined the timing of decolonisation' [107 *p. 139*].

SOME PROBLEMS WITH NATIONALIST INTERPRETATIONS

None the less, many historians of decolonisation remain wary of stressing the primacy of mass nationalism. This reflects a growing scepticism concerning the degree to which unified successor nations have been created from colonial rule. The problems which many African and Asian nations faced from the 1960s suggested that they were often artificial creations riven by ethnic, religious and regional divisions [115]. Decolonising territories remained heterogeneous and divided societies in which imperial policy, whether intentionally or unintentionally, could still play a significant role in dictating events.

Competing Nationalisms

Sizeable groups within particular colonies often did not embrace nationalism, and provided their own competing, counter- or subnationalism. Nationalist parties frequently had to contend with powerful regional leaders and allegiances. In India, regionalism was compounded by religious divisions between Muslims and Hindus [6 *p. 100*]. Congress's three great waves of mass agitation and civil disobedience – after the First World War, in the early 1930s and during the Second World War – may have forced constitutional concessions from the British and may have hampered British plans for an orderly transfer of power. But they also increasingly stimulated Muslim fears that a Congress India would be a Hindu India [108]. Gandhi was frequently unable to control his campaigns of peaceful non-co-operation as they descended into violence not only against the British but also between Indian communities [86]. The *Raj's* denouement was punctuated by bloody communal rioting and mass migrations – in which up to one million people lost their lives – as the subcontinent was partitioned into Congress India and Muslim League Pakistan. In Nigeria, the anti-colonial front was fractured by the tendency of 'nationalist' politicians to emphasise ethnic and religious identity. Zik's NCNC – despite original intentions – slid into Igbo chauvinism while the Yoruba community in the west formed its own cultural and political organisations. Moreover, Zik failed to attract support from the northern Hausa-Fulani Muslims who continued to follow their Emirs in the Northern Peoples' Congress. In 1960 Nigeria achieved independence, but as a federal, and conspicuously artificial, 'nation' with clear signs of trouble ahead [10].

The Gold Coast provides another illuminating model: this time not as a guide to the strength of postwar, populist anti-colonialism but to the complexities and diversities of nationalism, as well as the scramble for power unleashed by terminal colonialism. The final years of decolonisation in the Gold Coast witnessed the rise of an anti-Nkrumah party, the National Liberation Movement, based on the kingdom of Ashanti. This movement ultimately succeeded in slowing down the decolonisation process by forcing the British government into demanding a third general election in 1956 as proof of the CPP's 'national' legitimacy. The Ashanti party was also joined by other regional, ethnic and religious groups to demand a federal constitution as a counter to the CPP as a party of non-aristocratic upstarts, and as a party dominated by southern Ghanaians [105; 106] [*Doc. 22*]. Meanwhile, many ex-soldiers in Ghana remained fiercely loyal to the British colonial administration [99].

Ethnic and regional tensions were further complicated in colonies and territories with entrenched and vociferous white-settler populations. Most notoriously, in Kenya and in Southern Rhodesia, a white African nationalism emerged in the course of the twentieth century which curiously blended empire loyalism with demands for self-government and, hence, control over black Africans. Necessarily, this was a very different vision from that espoused by 'native' African nationalists in east and central Africa. 'With the competing nationalisms of settler and native proving mutually inflammatory, the sheer cost of maintaining metropolitan control rapidly threatened to become prohibitive' [19 *p. 96*]. Kenya emerged as a black-dominated state in 1963. But in November 1965, Southern Rhodesia made a unilateral declaration of independence from the United Kingdom in an attempt to forestall progress towards black majority rule; causing severe embarrassment for British governments for the next fifteen years. Britain's preferred outcome – 'one man, one vote' – only emerged in

1980 as Southern Rhodesia became Zimbabwe [5; 12]. As Porter and Stockwell have shrewdly observed, 'it was not nationalism but *competing* nationalisms that both strained and often led to the abandonment of British plans for orderly transfer of power' [187, 2 *p. 50*]. The realities of nationalism were no more complex than in Malaya. In the course of the nineteenth and twentieth centuries mass Chinese and Indian immigration created a plural society in the Malay States. In such an atmosphere, Malayan politics took on a 'communal' rather than a 'national' orientation. To present the communist revolt of 1948 as a nationalist uprising is problematic since the MCP was largely a Chinese chauvinist organisation and did not appeal to the Malays. Moreover, British attempts to create a multiracial Malayan identity were frustrated, first, in mass Malay protests against the Malayan Union plan and, second, in the electoral failure of Dato Onn's multiracial Independence of Malaya Party. Instead, an uneasy alliance of communal parties – the United Malays National Organisation (UMNO), the Malayan Chinese Association (MCA) and the Malayan Indian Congress – came to power under a federal constitution in 1955 and led Malaya to complete independence in 1957. British ideals of multiracialism and common citizenship were severely compromised [50].

Moreover, there were deep divisions even within the separate Malayan communities. A Malay political culture and consciousness had emerged under colonial rule from the late-eighteenth century. But Milner's close 'interrogation' of Malay political writings has revealed a situation of ideological contestation between three distinct forms of community in Malay society: the sultanate, the Islamic congregation, and the Malay race. In a sense, the modern conception of a Malay community united by race, represented by the main Malay political party, UMNO, triumphed in the ideological struggle by the decolonisation era. But Islamic and monarchical allegiances were far from extinguished, meaning that 'even in the last years of the British presence, the character and value of [Malay] nationalism continued to be a matter of debate' [102 *p. 6*].

Among the Chinese population, the Communist Party appealed to the Chinese proletariat who retained their traditional dialect, culture and affinities. But clearly this was not attractive to the English-educated business and professional elite who formed the MCA in 1949. Meanwhile, the long-established Straits Chinese of Penang went so far as to seek secession from the Federation of Malaya and retention of their loyalist links with the British Empire [87].

Separatist movements, as Clive Christie tells us in the light of events in the former Yugoslavia and Soviet Union, should be taken more seriously by historians of decolonisation. Britain's other principal possession in Southeast Asia, Burma, was riven by ethnic, communist and regional rebellions from the time of independence in 1948 [87]. The Japanese occupation and its chaotic aftermath accelerated political development in Southeast Asia. But it also complicated nationalism through exacerbating ethnic tensions and intensifying the contests for power among communists, nationalists, and regionalists [111]. Hence, in the last stages of decolonisation several, conflicting 'imagined communities' often emerged in colonial societies. Nationalists were sometimes faced with scenarios where they had to contain nationalism as much as the imperialists, and in the post-colonial world there remained many marginalised and frustrated groups [19 *pp. 109–10*]. For example, in much of colonial Africa women had played an important role in nationalist agitations. Their aspirations, however, were rarely met in the independence era [1; 92].

The Role of Imperial Policy

Decolonisation should perhaps be seen as a 'struggle for who should rule' rather than a 'struggle against colonial rule'. '[T]he dichotomy of imperialism and nationalism is a poor guide to the realities of colonial politics' [6 *p. 101*]. Many nationalists who sought to lead former colonial states to independence came to realise that the trickiest hurdle in their path was not the British authorities but competing nationalists. Indeed, in the later stages of decolonisation partnerships were forged between dominant nationalist groups and British colonial officialdom, particularly where obstructive regional interests threatened to fragment the former colonial territory [6 *p. 104*]. For example, in Ghana, Nkrumah and his CPP ministers were forced to seek the aid of the governor, Sir Charles Arden-Clarke (as well as ministers and mandarins in London), to counter the intransigent regional forces of Ashanti and the Northern Territories. Indeed, Arden-Clarke was referred to in Ashanti as the 'CPP Propaganda Secretary' [105 *p. 258*]. In Malaya, meanwhile, the conservative Alliance co-operated with the British authorities in the suppression of radical anti-colonialism in the guise of the MCP [50]. Moreover, in the early 1950s, when colonial economic conditions dramatically improved following the Korean war commodity boom, and the British turned to conciliation with nationalist leaders, the postwar 'crisis of empire' petered out and nationalist movements lost their militant edge. In west Africa and Southeast Asia, at least, this allowed the British authorities to regain the initiative and ensure remarkable continuity between colonial and post-colonial states [96; 112].

It remains difficult to deny the role of British officials (whether 'on the spot' or in Whitehall) and politicians in stimulating colonial mobilisation. Decolonisation represented a complicated interaction between nationalism and imperialism. As Gallagher pointed out, 'In Africa, as in India, much of the impetus behind the mass parties came from the policies of the government itself'[8 *p. 148*]. Throughout Africa and Asia (and in European societies such as Cyprus) nationalist movements and insurgencies were products not of 'the *stasis* of the colonial presence, but of its dynamic' [11 p. 175]. This new pro-active colonialism was not only stimulated by the needs of British economic recovery but also the new requirements of international strategy in the Cold War. In the Middle East, for example, fear of Russian intrusion and the need for forward air bases to bomb the Soviet Union in event of war pointed to a continued, and sometimes expanded, military occupation [6 *p. 119*]. But this only served to provoke local nationalists; most notably in Egypt during the 1950s (see Chapter 6) and in Cyprus culminating in an insurgency war between 1955 and 1959 [95]. Similar processes had taken place in interwar India. Nationalism was stimulated as the *Raj* spread its tentacles from Delhi into local arenas as declining British military and economic power served only to highlight India's importance to the empire. The British opened up the Indian political system after the First World War – just as in Africa after the Second World War – to widen the basis of collaboration and so more effectively to exploit India [3; 18; 52; 101]. As the colonial state grew in India it broke down the barriers between locality, province and nation, and Indian nationalism emerged as 'a matching structure of politics' within the framework of British rule [110].

On closer inspection, historians of decolonisation have not necessarily underestimated the role of nationalism. Rather, anti-colonial pressures have been placed within a range of factors which determined decolonisation. The balance of factors (peripheral, metropolitan and international) varied with time and place [187]. Local pressures 'interlocked' with other 'constraints' on British actions [6 *pp. 107–8*]. The mere fact that the break-up of most of the empire occurred in a short time-span of twenty years between 1945 and 1965 suggests that other forces were at work besides nationalism. Territories at very different levels of political, social and economic development were plunged into independence in this period. Strikes, riots and insurgencies coincided with imperial intrusions and reassessments and, what concerns us in the next two chapters, international pressures [6; 187].

PART FOUR: INTERNATIONAL CHANGE AND DECOLONISATION

5 THE BRITISH EMPIRE IN THE NEW WORLD ORDER

THE INTERNATIONAL CONTEXT

It is difficult for historians of decolonisation to ignore the changed international environment after the Second World War. The period between about the late 1940s and the late 1980s was unique in the sense that it was dominated by two rival superpowers – the United States and the Soviet Union. Before the war, international relations had been dominated by several competing great powers but in the postwar, bi-polar era the world divided into two opposing camps in what was labelled the Cold War. In this, the 'international colonial system' was superseded and eventually dismantled. The colonial system came into being between about 1880 and 1914 and survived only slightly modified by the First World War. It was characterised by a system of co-operation rather than rivalry between the major European powers. International treaties demarcated each colonial territory as the exclusive 'sphere of influence' of a particular imperial power. Hence, Britain could rely on no other major power interfering in its colonial affairs. Decolonisation can thus be explained by the postwar marginalisation of this colonial system in world politics [120; 129]. One Colonial Office mandarin apparently recognised the trend as early as 1942 when he declared: 'Nineteenth century conceptions of empire are dead' [129 p. 37].

The dramatically changed international landscape after 1945 is most clearly evinced by the colossal economic and military might of the United States and the Soviet Union relative to Britain and its empire [125]. Stimulated by a massive increase in wartime spending, American Gross National Product (GNP) rose from $88.6 billion in 1939 to $135 billion in 1945. The United States was the only power to gain economically from the Second World War. Between 1940 and

1944 industrial output in the United States rose by 15 per cent a year. At the end of the conflict, the United States owned two-thirds of the world's gold bullion, one-half of its manufacturing production, one-half of its supply of shipping while supplying one-third of its exports. 'Economically, the world was its oyster' [125 *p. 358*]. Global economic supremacy was reflected in American military muscle: at the end of the war the armed forces could boast 12.5 million personnel (7.5 million overseas). The American navy now dwarfed its British counterpart. The American airforce commanded the air with over two thousand heavy bombers and, above all, a monopoly of atomic weapons. The massive projection of American economic power overseas was accompanied by the establishment of a mass of military bases and security pacts which, by the 1950s, spanned the globe [125].

But the Americans squared up against a formidable opponent. Through its victory against Nazi Germany, the Soviet Union had extended its own boundaries, and the immediate postwar years witnessed the development of an informal empire of satellite states in Eastern Europe. The Soviet economy had been devastated by the war, and the highly centralised command economy would prove itself to be hopelessly inefficient. Nevertheless, the Soviet Union's imposing military might could not be ignored. The Red Army was reduced by two-thirds after the war. But it could still boast some 175 divisions, supported by tens of thousands of front-line tanks and aircraft. Combined with the vast Soviet navy, this was the largest defence complex in the world which, in the aftermath of the Second World War, underwent a thoroughgoing modernisation programme. In 1949 the West was horrified to learn that the Russians had successfully exploded their first atomic bomb [125].

Britain had ended the war at the victor's table but, in contrast to the United States, faced the peace in impecunious circumstances. Postwar Britain faced a colossal balance of payments deficit combined with a weakened industrial base while still maintaining enormous overseas commitments in the empire and beyond. Economic recovery was dependent upon the massive loan Lord Keynes secured in Washington in 1945 as well as Marshall Plan aid after 1947. By 1950 Britain's total GNP was less than one-fifth of the United States's, and just over one-half of the Soviet Union's. Britain's international eclipse was all the more marked in military capacity. In 1950 the United States's defence bill came to $14.5 billion and it had 1.38 million persons under arms; the Soviet Union spent $15.5 billion on forces totalling 4.3 million personnel. This was far ahead of anything Britain could muster with expenditures of just $2.3 billion and 680,000 personnel

[125]. The marginalisation of Britain in international affairs was heightened by the new 'strategic landscape' dominated not only by air power, but also nuclear weapons and long-range delivery systems. The empire's traditional basis of power, in contrast, was at sea. The British Empire was still a powerful strategic entity, but the imperial system's continued existence was now dependent on the United States for both military and economic security [125; 127].

Not only was the empire economically and strategically outmoded: the Cold War was also an ideological battleground in which empires appeared intellectually obsolete. The war of independence against Britain in the late-eighteenth century was ingrained in American national mythology, and this revolutionary tradition tended to make Americans sympathetic towards colonial peoples seeking self-determination [63 *p. xl*]. The United States instinctively distanced itself from European imperialism in its search for the support of the Afro-Asian world. As one American State Department official observed in October 1956: 'colonial issues had become the principal battleground between East and West' and hence it was 'especially important to the US to adopt policies which would retain the sympathies of the colonial peoples' [182, 1 *p. 240*]. Indeed, colonialism was seen as a hindrance in uniting the 'free world' against Soviet aggression [*Doc. 23*]. In the global 'struggle for existence' the Americans came to believe – from the late 1940s – that the Soviet Union (sometimes in coalition with communist China) aimed at world domination; the United States had no choice but to halt communist expansionism by bolstering non-communist regions of the Third World. Thus Washington extended its policy of containment from Western Europe to Asia and Africa; a strategy which could easily impinge upon the interests of lesser 'middle powers' such as the British Empire [119]. There were also pressures for decolonisation from the requirements of American economic diplomacy: it was unlikely that the world's largest economy would now be prepared to tolerate closed colonial economic systems, such as the sterling area, which secured markets and raw materials for the European imperialists [125].

On the reverse side of the coin, was the anti-colonial ideology emanating from the Soviet Union. The great theorist and leader of the Bolshevik Revolution of 1917, V. I. Lenin, believed that nationalist movements in the colonial world could become the allies of the European working class in its revolutionary struggle against capitalism and imperialism. The victory of the proletariat in Europe would also bring about the collapse of the European empires. Indeed, many nationalist leaders looked to the Soviet Union as a source of revolutionary inspiration and as an alternative model of socialist modernisation. By the mid-1950s, the Soviets projected themselves as allies of emerging nations, and began a policy of both military and economic aid as a deliberate attempt to isolate the American-led, 'capitalist-imperialist' bloc [132].

In addition, the British had to contend with the international institutions of the 'new world order'. The United Nations (UN) was formed in 1945 with a wider remit and membership than its predecessor, the League of Nations. (For example, the UN included the United States from its outset.) 'The UN was to assist the rise of new states, themselves the result of decolonization, which in their turn became involved in the international diplomacy of subsequent decolonizations' [19 *p. 69*]. Embarrassingly for the British, the 'anti-colonial bloc' in the UN was led by India, and during the 1950s Nehru became the leader of the 'non-aligned movement' of independent Third World countries. As skilful players on the UN stage, Indian diplomats provided a sustained critique of imperialism [*Doc. 24*]. 'Although membership of the UN seemed to produce some overall advantages to Britain, handling it proved frustrating and hard work in the colonial field' [31 *p. xxiv*]. The independence of Ghana in 1957 added another anti-colonial voice at the UN, and Kwame Nkrumah was to become a key figure in the pan-Africanist Organisation of African Unity (established in 1963) which supported nationalist politicians against the European imperial powers. Indeed, 'the more that colonial policy was "fulfilled" in the creation of new states, the more the attacks on that same policy gained international voice' [63 *p. xlv*].

AMERICAN ANTI-COLONIALISM IN WAR AND PEACE

The Conflicting Aims of Britain and the United States During the Second World War

The Second World War is notable for the conflicting colonial aims of Britain and the United States. America joined Britain in the worldwide conflict following the Japanese bombing of Pearl Harbor in December 1941; the Anglo-Saxons were, however, only ever 'allies of a kind' [136]. There was a long tradition of anti-colonialism in American foreign policy which predated the bi-polar conflict with the Soviet Union. In the aftermath of the First World War, President Woodrow Wilson ensured that the former German and Turkish territories would not be re-annexed as colonies but instead administered as 'mandates' under the newly formed League of Nations. In the

British Empire territories such as Palestine and Tanganyika were held as 'sacred trusts of civilisation'. Wilson's ideas were further developed by America's President during the Second World War, Franklin D. Roosevelt* [127]. There is no doubting Roosevelt's anti-colonialism: like Wilson before him, Roosevelt regarded empires as a threat to world peace. The colonies of Europe would be placed under international administration or 'trusteeship' after the war, and, although decolonisation was to be a gradual process, Roosevelt was certain that self-determination and independence was the ultimate goal [127; 138]. Roosevelt 'should be regarded as one of the fathers of the post-war world of politically independent nations' [127 p. 5].

The contrast in colonial outlook between Roosevelt and Britain's wartime Prime Minister, Winston Churchill, was marked. Churchill was an unreconstructed Victorian imperialist; the British Empire was his 'religion'; and his politically incorrect references to the Chinese as 'Chinks', for example, greatly irritated Roosevelt [127]. For Churchill, the Atlantic Charter's pronouncements of August 1941 on 'self-determination' only referred to Nazi-conquered Europe; Roosevelt believed self-determination should be applied to colonial territories as well. The loss of empire in the Far East was central in focusing American anti-colonialism. The ease with which the Japanese had defeated the European empires in eastern Asia suggested something rather rotten at the heart of colonialism, and the future of the occupied colonies became dependent on the United States war effort against the Japanese. For the British, meanwhile, American ideas on 'trusteeship' were equated with the dismemberment of empire and were seen as a cover for informal American expansionism [127; 136].

American critiques of empire also concentrated on Britain's problems in South Asia, especially after August 1942 with the 'Quit India' campaign led by Congress [127; 137]. An 'Open letter to the people of England' published by *Life* magazine in October 1942 warned that: 'If your strategists are planning a war to hold the British Empire together they will sooner or later find themselves strategizing all alone... In the light of what you are doing in India, how do you expect us to talk about "principles" and look our soldiers in the eye?' [128 p. 399]. In response to the anti-British sentiment of many American politicians and journalists, Roosevelt proposed the extension of the Atlantic Charter to Asia. He argued that the political impasse in India could be solved by granting self-government. For officials in the State Department, political independence would give Indians something to fight for in the war against Japan. To the British, American attitudes seemed hopelessly simplistic. British pro-empire propaganda attempted to stress the realities of much of the dependent empire which, it was argued, simply could not cope with independence without extended and gradual political, economic and social development. But such arguments were regarded by the Americans as biased, imperial self-interest [127; 138].

The British were regarded by the Americans as more progressive than their European imperial counterparts (especially the French). None the less, the British Empire was still 'an *Empire* with all of the inherent evils of European colonialism. ... The pace for self-government and measures for education, health, and welfare had to be accelerated' [127 *p. 20*]. One means of achieving colonial reform, the Americans believed, was through international administration of the colonies in which the United States would play a central role. To his death in April 1945 Roosevelt maintained that the biggest threat to world peace after the war would not emanate from the Soviet Union but from the continued existence of the British Empire [127]. 'A fitful and most uncomfortable sleeping partner had joined the imperial board of directors' [47 *p. 54*].

Roosevelt's romantic anti-colonialism was given further pertinence by more hard-headed and self-interested economic notions within the United States State Department, Treasury, and business community. During the war, economic internationalists, such as Secretary of State Cordell Hull, claimed that the global conflict had been largely caused by protectionist economic policies – such as tariff barriers and restrictive access to raw materials – on the part of the major powers. There were, therefore, calls to dismantle the empire-Commonwealth trading bloc. Meanwhile, influential elements in the American business community were pushing for 'economic expansion' to sustain wartime levels of production in the postwar world. British officials were alarmed by the penetration of American commercial interests into traditional British business preserves, such as the Middle East, India and west Africa, during the war. Furthermore, the American military sought control of strategic raw materials – such as oil, rubber and metal ores – many of which were to be found within British colonial boundaries [33; 125; 138]. The institutions of the new free-trading international economic order – underwritten by the American economy – emerged during and immediately after the war; the International Monetary Fund (IMF) and the International Bank for Reconstruction and Development (the World Bank) surfaced from the Bretton Woods Agreement of 1944 while the General Agreement on Tariffs and Trade was signed in 1947. These economically liberal organisations were instinctively hostile to trading regimes such as the sterling area which were based on fixed exchange rates and trade preferences [125]. Indeed, the war and its aftermath was not necessarily characterised by an American ethical, anti-imperial crusade. 'Revisionists' have argued that American insistence on decolonisation was motivated by economic self-interest, and that 'trusteeship' simply hid the reality: American informal, economic imperialism [126].

Postwar American Pressures to Decolonise

In the immediate aftermath of war it seemed quite likely that the Americans would take advantage of British economic weakness to dismantle empire, and establish a system of international colonial trusteeship. Britain, faced with alarming problems of economic revival, was dependent on the United States to underwrite and bolster the empire [130]. The Attlee government came up against a 'forbidding' set of developments in United States foreign policy [138 *p. 106*]. Most worrying was America's economic diplomacy: in return for a dollar loan of £3.75 billion, the British were forced to make the pound convertible with the dollar within twelve months. In effect, this meant the end of the sterling area's protectionist currency and trade arrangements [130].

Certainly, American pressure was to have a profound influence on early British decolonisation. The Americans did not play a significant role in the final stages of Indian decolonisation and partition between 1947 and 1948 [128]. However, Bevin's conclusion by 1947 that American support was unlikely in Palestine – given the strength of the Jewish lobby in Washington – played a large part in Britain's rather inglorious withdrawal in 1948 [23; 36; 43; 131]. The United States was, at the same time, emerging as the protector of Arab nationalism against British and French imperial designs in the Middle East. In this, the Soviet Union was regarded as an anti-imperial ally rather than an expansionist enemy [138]. Furthermore, the Americans had carried through their own decolonisation in their only colony of substance, the Philippines. Roosevelt had agreed with Filipino nationalists in 1934 that the Philippines would become independent in 1946 and, despite the intervening Japanese occupation, this promise was kept [167].

EMPIRE AND COLD WAR

'Empire Preserved'

But, as the Cold War emerged as the dominant reality of international politics in the years between 1947 and 1951, 'competition between the two superpowers came to the rescue of the Empire' [130 *p. 467*].

By the end of 1947 there emerged a convergence of views among diplomats, politicians and military figures on both sides of the Atlantic concerning the dangers presented by the Soviet Union [138]. Under the presidency of Harry S. Truman, American foreign policy objectives shifted from imperial dismemberment to the containment of Soviet expansion. In the Middle East, the Americans now appreciated Britain's traditional and crucial role in blocking Russian imperialism. Meanwhile, Washington softened its attitude towards the sterling area. In seeking to facilitate Western Europe's rapid economic rejuvenation and, thus, reduce the appeal of Soviet-backed communist parties, Washington now came to accept protectionist colonial arrangements even though these denied markets for American export industries. Marshall Plan funds from 1947 bolstered the European empires and encouraged the maximisation of colonial export production to earn and save dollars essential for metropolitan recovery. It was also appreciated in Washington that politically stable colonies were vital for the supply of strategic raw materials [19; 130].

Moreover, as the Cold War spread to Asia – with the Maoist triumph in China by the end of 1949 followed by Chinese intervention in the Korean War at the end of 1950 – Washington relied on the British (and the French) Empire to block Sino-Soviet expansion in Southeast Asia [130]. In the case of British Malaya, for example, the State Department appreciated by 1950 that the British were fighting a war against communist insurgents assumed to be the agents of Moscow and Beijing. At the same time, the colonial regime was earning vital dollars from Malayan rubber and tin exports which propped up Britain's domestic economic position and, hence, Britain's ability to assist in the resistance of communism in Europe [135]. The Americans still 'stood committed to decolonisation; yet they had no wish to alienate their NATO allies by hurrying the pace' [121 *p. 286*].

For Louis and Robinson, empire was temporarily 'preserved' as part of an 'Anglo-American coalition'. American sustenance stabilised the British balance of payments and, hence, maintained British power overseas in the 'democratic cause of saving the global free market from communist annexation' [130 *p. 493*]. Anglo-American collaboration came to the fore in Britain's informal empire in the Middle East. In Iran the August 1953 *coup* overthrew the radical nationalist Musaddiq who had nationalised the massive British oil refinery at Abadan in 1951. To prevent Iran becoming a Soviet satellite, this *coup* was fostered by British and American intelligence services and it successfully restored the powers of the pro-Western Shah. American military aid underpinned the Shah's regime. For their trouble, the Americans were awarded 33 per cent of the Iranian oil market in the settlement of 1954 [118; 130].

The Revival of American Anti-Colonialism in the mid-1950s

Yet, Anglo-American collaboration in empire went through a rocky period during the mid-1950s. With the exception of the Iranian *coup*, both Prime Ministers Churchill and Eden attempted to play a more independent role. American and British aims began to diverge. By the mid-1950s, the logic of American anti-communism shifted from support for West European allies to support for moderate nationalist movements in the colonial empires. The recovery of the European economies, particularly after the Korean war boom of the early 1950s, had reduced their dependence on colonial markets and supplies. More importantly, the Americans had come to view controlled decolonisation as an essential element in Cold War strategy; the continuance of European imperialism would only drive nationalist movements into the arms of the Soviet Union. '[A]nti-colonialism was one issue on which the United States could comfortably align with the newly emerging nations' [124 *p. 115*] [*Doc. 23*].

Anglo-American friction reached its peak in the Middle East, culminating in the Suez débâcle of 1956 (see Chapter 6). In contrast to Churchill and his Cabinet during the Iranian crisis, Eden and his Cabinet were not prepared to play second fiddle to the Americans in Egypt. President Eisenhower – through financial pressure – vetoed the Anglo-French military effort to overthrow Egyptian President Nasser for fear of the whole Middle East and North Africa coming under Soviet influence as a result of imperial clumsiness. The Americans effectively insisted that their major ally now 'give priority' to the Cold War over its empire [130 *p. 480*].

The Revival of the Anglo-American Coalition After Suez

After Suez, the new British Prime Minister, Macmillan, worked much more closely with the Americans than either Churchill or Eden before him. The Anglo-American 'coalition' was resurrected [11; 12; 130]. Beloff suggests that the Americans manoeuvred the British out of empire, but without taking full responsibility for the political chaos and economic decline that often ensued in the aftermath of premature withdrawal [117]. For Louis and Robinson, however, after 1957 the British increasingly worked in concert, rather than in conflict, with the Americans to manage decolonisation and so keep Soviet influence in the emerging Third World at a minimum. There was no 'conspiracy' to take over the British Empire and replace it with American 'neo-colonialism': 'American influence expanded by imperial default and nationalist invitation' [130 *p. 495*]. The argument is that on both sides of the Atlantic it was now understood that if Soviet subversion in the Third World was to be prevented, decolonisation led by moderate nationalists should be promoted. To the American 'official mind' political independence combined with an injection of outside resources would incline newly independent countries towards the West. Hence, the Eisenhower Doctrine of 1957 allocated up to $200 million of aid a year for the Middle East, while the Anglo-American invasions of Jordan and Lebanon in 1958 confirmed British acceptance of American leadership of the 'free world' in the region [16; 130].

By the later 1950s British officials and politicians did appear to be prioritising Cold War considerations in their decolonisation strategies. An influential interdepartmental report of 1959 – which was discussed with American officials – concluded that 'if ... we are too intransigent in opposing African aspirations ... we run the risk of ... provoking the African States when they finally achieve independence ... to turn more readily towards the Soviet Union' [*Doc. 25*]. Friendly nationalists would provide a 'barrier' to Soviet entry. But this new informal empire would also have to be cemented by Western economic and military aid; otherwise 'the Governments of the new States may be compelled to turn to the Soviet Union for the assistance which they will certainly need' [*Doc. 25*]. The bulk of this aid would have to come from the United States [130]. Most famously, Harold Macmillan's 'Wind of Change' speech in Cape Town in February 1960 argued that resistance to decolonisation would only serve to drive colonial populations into the arms of the communist bloc [*Doc. 26*]. But, while control was relinquished in west Africa, until about 1960 British officials and politicians believed that in east Africa, if not in central Africa, empire would survive for another decade if not longer [130].

The Congo Crisis, 1960–3

According to Louis and Robinson, however, these complacent timetables in 'settler' Africa were to be ditched in the light of Anglo-American and Cold War exigencies. The international repercussions of the Congo crisis between 1960 and 1963 are crucial to understanding why Britain abandoned the white settlers in favour of African majority rule and swift independence in east and southern Africa [130]. The sudden Belgian scuttle from colonial responsibility threatened the disintegration of the Congo in which radical nationalists vied for Soviet support. The Cold War had finally arrived in Africa, and the fallout from superpower intervention threatened the whole continent [123]. Hence, Louis and Robinson argue that the 'supreme test' of Anglo-American 'solidarity' – through the United Nations – was to successfully 'hold the Congo together' and keep it aligned to the West [130 *p. 490*]. As Holland also stresses: '[A] balkanized central Africa would maximize the chances of a successful Russian penetration into the area. ... [W]estern strategic concerns had a great deal with Congolese reconsolidation' [12 *p. 189*].

The threat of a whole host of Congo-style embroilments in other parts of the continent convinced the British that their obligations in Africa now had to be scaled down as quickly as possible before the international costs of decolonisation became unbearable. Given the Congo's crucial geopolitical position in the heart of Africa, the British believed that disorder, and hence Soviet influence, in the ex-Belgian territory could easily spill over its borders into Uganda, Tanganyika, Kenya and the Central African Federation [123]. It was better to leave too soon rather than too late and so build up reserves of goodwill and secure a pro-Western orientation in post-colonial states.

By the mid-1960s Britain's imperial epoch was at an end. The British, say Louis and Robinson, had fallen into line with American strategies of alliances with independent Third World countries, as opposed to outmoded colonial domination [130]. As D. C. Watt also notes, 'Macmillan, Macleod and the "Wind of Change", and the destruction of Lord Salisbury as the last of the imperialists, went down well in Washington' [138 *p. 135*].

INTERNATIONAL PRESSURES RECONSIDERED

The Limits of the Superpowers

But were the realities of the New World Order the exclusive or most important determinants of decolonisation after 1945? Dunbabin argues that the role of the superpowers in decolonisation has been exaggerated [122]. On a physical level, the Soviet Union 'had few openings to exert direct influence within the colonies' [122 *p. 62*]. It was not until the 1970s that naval expansion under Brezhnev's leadership allowed the Russians to support nationalist guerrilla armies in overseas theatres, for example during the Portuguese withdrawal from southern Africa [19 *p. 71*]. During the Second World War, Stalin* was concerned not to weaken his British allies. As a result, the Indian communists were instructed to support the British decision on

India's entry into the war against the opposition of Congress [132]! In the postwar era, Moscow remained relatively indifferent to colonial nationalism, and Communist parties (for example, in British Malaya) received little or no support. Soviet trade with much of the decolonising world remained negligible, and Russian strategists looked to land power in Europe rather than naval power overseas [121]. There were also ideological limitations on Soviet influence in the Third World. Bolshevik anti-colonialism had been severely compromised as early as the 1920s when the Soviets reconquered, rather than freed, the former Tsarist empire in the Caucasus and Central Asia. As put forward by Stalin, only nations of substantial demographic and geographic dimensions were regarded as capable of achieving independence. This, of course, legitimised the multinational Soviet state. Nationalism was, after all, a potentially disintegrative phenomenon within the Soviet Union itself given that less than 60 per cent of the Soviet population was Russian [19]. Stalin's view of anti-colonial nationalism was also coloured by experiences in China before the Second World War. Despite Soviet political and military aid, Chiang Kai-shek's Guomindang – in its campaign for national unification and independence during the 1920s and 1930s – turned against its former communist allies. Chiang's 'betrayal' was not forgotten: postwar nationalist leaders such as Nehru and Nkrumah were classified as 'bourgeois nationalists'; 'imperialist stooges' who remained the neo-colonial agents of capitalist imperialism. Stalin clung stubbornly to the doctrine that a former colony could become truly independent only under communist rule [121; 132].

Following Stalin's death in 1953, but particularly after the aborted Anglo-French Suez invasion of 1956, Khrushchev* brought a new Soviet policy to the decolonising world. By the late-1950s/early-1960s it was believed that independence could be achieved by the 'bourgeoisie'. Communist parties in the Third World were now encouraged to form alliances with the 'national bourgeoisie' in the common struggle for the 'national democratic revolution' as the first stage in the proletarian revolution. Soviet diplomats now took a leading role in anti-colonial debates in the United Nations [121; 132]. But this often amounted to 'too little, too late' to have a direct bearing on decolonisation since the key decisions to transfer power, in the British Empire at least, had already been taken.

In comparison to the Soviets/Russians, the Americans were more pro-active 'anti-imperialists'. The intervention of the United States in Palestine in the 1940s and at Suez in 1956 had a crucial influence on the outcome of these decolonisation crises. But this is a 'shortlist' of 'overt' American intrusion into British colonial affairs, suggesting that 'decolonisation was primarily a question between the colonies and their metropolitan countries' [122 *p. 64*]. The British, it could be argued, had their own autonomous decolonisation agenda designed to retain economic and strategic influence in return for swift transfers of power to friendly nationalists. As such it is 'the British as much as the Americans [who] are responsible for the aftermath of instability and deprivation, civil and tribal war, famine, and even genocide' which has afflicted many post-colonial states [128 *p. 418*]. American Secretary of State, Cordell Hull, recalled in his memoirs that: 'At no time did we press Britain, France or the Netherlands for an immediate grant of self-government in the colonies' [cited in 119 *p. 174*]. Rather, American policy both during and after the war tended to bolster rather than undermine the British imperial system. In India, the Roosevelt administration was frightened by the prospects of revolution, and anti-colonialism had to be weighed up against the Anglo-American alliance and victory in the war. Gandhi had not helped his cause in Washington by refusing to assist in the conflict with Germany and then Japan [128; 137]. After the war, the American military continued to believe that Britain's withdrawal from its colonies would only create areas of instability and, 'When the threat of Russia became ominous, the watchword "security" began to eclipse "independence"' [127 *p. 568*].

American anti-colonialism in the Cold War was superseded by what were regarded as more important considerations, notably anti-communism and international stability [119]. In 1958, for example, Assistant Secretary of State, C. Burke Elbrick, advised the Senate Foreign Relations Committee that, 'Premature independence and irresponsible nationalism may present grave dangers to dependent peoples' [119 *p. 175*]. While American influence in Pacific Asia and the Middle East was expanding, Africa remained an unknown quantity to most Americans. Until the Kennedy administration, the continent was viewed simply as a 'colonial appendage of Western Europe' [121 *p. 285*]. In 1958 the State Department's Bureau of African Affairs came into being, and eventually a number of consulates were replaced by full-blown embassies. Loans and grants now flowed towards the successor states [121]. But, like the Soviet push into Africa after 1956, this greater American effort in Africa came long after the main decisions on decolonisation had been taken in Britain.

The accession of the youthful John F. Kennedy to the presidency in 1960 brought a flurry of statements, such as support for the UN Declaration on Colonialism, which seemed to suggest a shift of emphasis in American foreign policy. But this was largely rhetoric: in Africa, for example, American policy remained conditioned by the exigencies of Cold War strategy [133]. The United States proved 'very selective in its choice of nationalist clients in the Third World. ... Even in the absence of open communist support, radical nationalists were often suspected of communist leanings; they were perceived as ... serving the interests of communism by creating instability and aligning themselves with the Soviet Union' [124 *p. 111*]. American strategy in the colonial world was increasingly to 'redirect' nationalism rather than complete emancipation [119 *p. 161*].

America's own decolonisation of the Philippines served not only as an important example of 'anti-colonialism' to the world but also the need for controlled and managed decolonisation. The Magsaysay regime in the Philippines during the 1950s was the model 'independent' government for the Americans. It was violently anti-communist and spoke of 'positive nationalism' in close alliance with the United States. The treaties signed on independence guaranteed American economic and military interests in the archipelago. As a consequence, Filipino independence, it could be argued, was always qualified. But to American thinking any larger measure of autonomy was dangerously pro-Soviet [19; 119; 167].

American anti-colonialism, then, was largely rhetorical. It was the bogey of *possible* American intervention rather than direct demands from Washington that in part led London to modernise colonial economies and democratise colonial administrations [127; 129]. There is little evidence of a threat from a new American economic imperialism either. It was recognised that United States industry was heavily dependent on Third World raw material supplies. Yet, it was really only in the case of Middle Eastern oil that American multinational companies were prepared to commit large capital resources for development in the 1950s. Despite government encouragement – on both sides of the Atlantic – few American firms were prepared to risk investments in the politically unstable and economically underdeveloped crumbling empire. When American businesses invested and traded overseas they developed links with the politically stable, culturally familiar, and affluent industrialised nations of the West [119; 121].

Nor was the empire always dismantled by a cosy Anglo-American 'coalition'. The 'special relationship' was often transitory. The British and the Americans did co-operate in the decolonisation of the former Italian colony of Libya as a means of blocking Soviet expansion into the Mediterranean and Africa; in exchange for independence in 1951 the new state leased bases to the British and the Americans [128]. But, in the Middle East – even after the Suez crisis of 1956 – rivalries continued between British and American diplomats and oil companies [122]. Moreover, by the later 1960s, the American elite was mortified by the final scaling down of Britain's extra-European commitments. In 1968 the Wilson government announced the withdrawal of British forces 'East of Suez' i.e. from Malaysia, Singapore, the Indian Ocean and the Persian Gulf. The British cutbacks were seen as a betrayal given America's costly embroilment at the time in Vietnam [138] [*Doc. 27*].

The 'real opening' for American and Soviet penetration of the Third World 'did not come until after independence' [122 *p. 64*]. American-Soviet rivalry in the Third World only became manifest from the mid-1960s when Soviet military spending started to exceed that of the United States. The Soviets now made their power felt in areas like the Middle East, Africa and Southeast Asia; once exclusively dominated by the West. Even so, in Africa, the Soviets and their allies still confined themselves to training guerrillas and subsidising pro-Soviet organisations; only after 1975 did the Soviets intervene directly in southern Africa [121 *pp. 292–3*].

The Limits of International Organisations

Meanwhile, President Roosevelt's ideas on international administration of colonial territories came to very little in practice. At the Allied Conference at Yalta in early 1945 the trusteeship system was limited to the ex-German, ex-Turkish and ex-Italian colonies. Britain was never forced to place its colonies under this system. The San Francisco Conference in April 1945 drew up the new UN Charter. This was committed to such lofty, high ideals as 'equal rights' between nations and 'self-determination of peoples'. But, significantly, the term 'self-government' was substituted for 'independence' in Chapter XI of the UN Charter which covered non-self-governing territories. A Trusteeship Council was formed as part of the UN to supervise the former League of Nations mandates, such as Palestine and Tanganyika in the British Empire. In practice, however, this was little different from the prewar system. If UN delegations wished to visit Palestine or Tanganyika they could only do so if invited by Britain [19; 127; 129].

Indeed, the UN's contribution to British decolonisation proved rather illusory and, at times, contradictory. The General Assembly of the UN had declared in 1960 that, 'All peoples have the right of self-determination'; 'lack of preparedness should never serve as a pretext for delaying independence' [122 p. 458]. In the later stages of decolonisation, then, UN opinion 'probably helped persuade metropolitan countries to extend the process to the smaller colonies they had originally regarded as "non-viable", and to strategic territories whose retention they had previously regarded as essential' [122 *p. 458*]. Yet, in 1963, when Britain announced that the Borneo territories would become independent but only as part of a federation with Malaya, the UN acquiesced. This despite the fact that the British Cobbold Commission had earlier found limited enthusiasm amongst the peoples of Sabah and Sarawak for Malaysian federation [122; 134]. In the Middle East, on the other hand, the UN's Special Committee on Colonialism determined to block British designs for incorporating Aden colony into the South Arabian Federation. None the less, British policy prevailed and Aden began its ill-fated merger with the Federation in 1963 [116; 122]. Up to the mid-1950s, at least, British diplomats at the UN proved remarkably adept at preventing or side-stepping debates on colonial questions [63]. Likewise, the pan-Africanist Organisation of African Unity imposed little pressure to decolonise since it acknowledged that Britain had already set in train measures to bring about colonial self-determination [10].

International Pressures in the Context of Metropolitan and Colonial Changes

Moreover, international pressures on the British Empire only intersected and interconnected with metropolitan and colonial changes. Macmillan's 'wind of change' in eastern and southern Africa after 1960 was partially influenced by international considerations such as the need to sustain the revived Anglo-American partnership and ensure a pro-Western or, at least, politically neutral Africa. But other factors also have to be taken into consideration: notably, Macmillan's eye on the progressive, younger electorate at home, the dramatic shift in Belgian policy in the Congo, and the French failure to suppress nationalism in Algeria [74].

As Louis and Robinson skilfully argued in 1982, the survival of the British imperial system depended on three factors: (1) that colonial peoples acquiesced with British rule; (2) that the politicians and voters in the metropole accepted colonial commitments on economic and ethical grounds; and that (3) the empire was recognised by international powers and organisations. Accordingly, any single-cause explanation of decolonisation will be simplistic. 'Colonial Office planners ultimately concluded that there could be no resolution of the tensions – international, metropolitan, and colonial – other than by swift transfers of power' [129 *p. 55*]. As Darwin concludes, the Second World War 'produced a dangerous conjuncture of international, domestic and colonial pressures, whose effects were mutually reinforcing' [6 *p. 120*].

6   SUEZ 1956: DID IT MATTER?

EVENT WRIT LARGE

In 1956 American pressure stopped the Anglo-French military expedition to overthrow Egyptian President Nasser, and denationalise the Suez Canal, dead in its tracks. This international intervention in a late-colonial episode is often seen as a great watershed, apocalyptically heralding the end of imperial statehood for Britain (and France). The repercussions, it has been argued, were not just felt in Egypt itself; American actions at Suez speeded up the process of decolonisation everywhere [150].

THE CRISIS

The Importance of Egypt and the Suez Canal

The Suez canal from its construction in 1869 occupied an essential position in the British imperial system, linking the Mediterranean with the Red Sea. As Anthony Eden, Prime Minister at the time of the 1956 Crisis, told the House of Commons back in 1929: 'If the Suez Canal is our back door to the East, it is the front door to Europe of Australia, New Zealand and India. ... [I]t is ... the swing-door of the British Empire, which has got to keep continually revolving if our communications are to be what they should' [149 p. 7].

The majority of the Suez Canal Company's shares were held by Britain and France (in a combination of both government and private holdings). Safeguarding this strategic asset was the principal motive for Britain's occupation of Egypt in 1882. Forty years later, Egypt regained its independence but this was conditional upon continued British control of Egypt's foreign and military affairs to safeguard the canal through which passed Britain's trade to and from the Middle East, India, the Far East and Australasia. The Anglo-Egyptian Treaty of 1936 established Britain's position in the Suez Canal Zone, allowed for the stationing of 10,000 troops in Egypt during peacetime, and confirmed Egypt's pivotal position in Britain's 'informal' Middle Eastern empire. The Suez Canal Base – the largest military base in the world – played a crucial role in the Second World War, supplying the Middle East, North Africa, and southern Europe [183; 185].

Britain's continued presence in Egypt, especially after the withdrawal from India, was regarded as central to any postwar revitalisation of imperial power and the preservation of great power status. The Suez base was central to the defence of the Middle East and, hence, to safeguard oil; to provide bases to bomb the Soviet Union; to prevent a Soviet incursion into Africa; to preserve trade links and sea communications; and 'to retain the prestige inherent in an imperial global role' [147 *p. 46*]. As part of the Attlee government's grand strategy of 'partnership' with Arab states, the British hoped after 1948 to reinvigorate the 1936 Treaty through a Middle Eastern Command. This, it was reasoned, would bring together Egypt and other Middle Eastern states, under British leadership and with American support, to form a regional security system *à la* NATO [144; 155].

Challenges to Britain's Position in Egypt

However, the British presence was increasingly resented by Egyptians, especially given Britain's perceived betrayal of the Arabs during the withdrawal from Palestine, followed by the creation of the Jewish state of Israel. In 1951 the Egyptian government ditched the 1936 Treaty and refused to join the Middle East Command. Meanwhile, Egyptian nationalists ambushed British troops in the Canal Base, and in January 1952 rioters in the capital Cairo burnt British property and killed eight foreigners. Responding to the popular mood, Free Officers in the military toppled Britain's traditional 'collaborator' in Egypt, King Farouk [155]. One of these young army nationalists, Colonel Gamal Abdel Nasser, became Prime Minister of Egypt in 1954, deposing General Mohammed Neguib.

British designs in Egypt (and the Middle East generally) were also under increasing pressure from international scrutiny in the guise of the United States. This was particularly so after January 1953 when Dwight D. Eisenhower* became the new President in Washington and appointed John Foster Dulles* as his Secretary of State. The Eisenhower administration abandoned the British concept of a Middle Eastern Command based on Egypt and proposed instead an American-backed 'Northern Tier' defence system from Turkey to Pakistan as a means of containing the Soviet threat [151]. At the same time, anxious to guide Egyptian nationalism along pro-Western lines, the

Americans – in contrast to the British – had established links with Nasser and the Free Officers [154; 155].

Washington urged the Churchill government to conclude a new Anglo-Egyptian Treaty in October 1954 which looked forward to British military evacuation from the Canal Zone by June 1956 (although the British could re-enter the Base in the event of war or threat of war). The British now shifted their policy in the Middle East away from Egypt – a process which may have begun as early as 1951. In the new era of thermo-nuclear weaponry the massive concentration of forces at Suez appeared as strategic insanity [24]. Lucas has suggested that the move away from Egypt involved developing an axis between Britain's closest allies in the region, Iraq and Jordan [151; 152]. Ashton, however, has emphasised that if there was an Iraqi-Jordanian policy this was only a part of Britain's foremost strategy, namely, the building up of pro-Western Iraq *alone* as leader of the Arab world. This policy was based upon the renewal of the Anglo-Iraqi alliance of 1930, and the bolstering of Iraq's anti-communist Prime Minister, Nuri Said [139].

None the less, Britain could not afford to ignore events in Egypt which took a turn for the worse in the course of 1955. The British-led, and Washington-backed, Baghdad Pact of 1955 brought Iraq and Turkey (and later Iran and Pakistan also) into an alliance of mutual defence against Soviet aggression. Egypt, against British wishes, refused to be sucked into this anti-communist bloc; the main threat to regional security for Egypt, after all, was not the Soviet Union but Israel. Western hopes for improved Egyptian-Israeli relations had been crippled in February 1955 when Israeli troops attacked an Egyptian military camp in Gaza. Furthermore, in September 1955, Nasser completed an arms deal with Czechoslovakia (a satellite of the Soviet Union), and increasingly projected Egypt as an alternative leader to Britain and the United States in the Arab world [185].

These unfortunate developments were not necessarily the last straw for Anglo-American interests in Egypt; it was still possible that Nasser would play a neutralist role in the Middle East. The Aswan High Dam – a project essential for Egypt's economic development – was now seized upon as a means of bringing Nasser back into the Western fold. The dam's dependence on Anglo-American – principally American – finance for its construction could be used as a lever to insist upon an Egyptian-Israeli peace agreement; thus allowing full concentration on Soviet expansion as the fundamental threat to regional stability [185].

However, Western relations with Egypt declined further as a result of other British plans for the Middle East. Foreign Secretary, Harold

Macmillan, attempted to bring Britain's long-term ally, Jordan, into the Baghdad Pact. Nasser, seeking to extend influence into the British-protected Middle East, financed public demonstrations in Jordan's capital Amman which forced Britain's collaborator, King Hussein, to dismiss his British military adviser, General Glubb, in March 1956. According to Lucas, 'Britain's entire defence strategy was now in jeopardy' [185 *p. 24*]. Events in Jordan also served to intensify Eden's personal hatred of the Colonel. Meanwhile, American plans for the Middle East were scuppered by March 1956. An Egyptian-Israeli agreement had been abandoned in the light of the intransigence of Nasser and Israeli Prime Minister, David Ben-Gurion. Hence, Britain and the United States agreed a joint strategy for Egypt. The plan, known as *Omega*, would destabilise the Nasser regime 'through propaganda and a series of economic and political measures' [153 *p. 27*]. At this stage, the Anglo-American 'coalition' in the Middle East was 'revived and ready to strike' [185 *p. 30*].

Responding to mounting political pressures in Washington, the Eisenhower administration withdrew American funding for the Aswan Dam. In retaliation against 'Western imperialism', Nasser nationalised the Suez Canal Company on 26 July 1956 (cleverly in the aftermath of the British military departure from the Suez base). This was potentially a huge threat to the British imperial system, not least because the canal carried from the Persian Gulf some two-thirds of Western Europe's oil [130]. Moreover, this was oil which could be bought from sterling companies, thus avoiding expenditure of scarce dollars [139]. As one Bank of England official warned, Egyptian nationalisation 'imperils the survival of the UK and the Commonwealth, and represents a very great danger to sterling' [148 *p. 215*].

The military expedition and its failure

Following the nationalisation, the British prepared a military expedition 'to bring about the fall of Nasser and create a government in Egypt which will work satisfactorily with ourselves and other powers' [130 *p. 479*]. Eden's strategy of military intervention received strong support from Harold Macmillan, now Chancellor of the Exchequer. Macmillan argued that Nasser could block the Suez canal; if that happened a massive American loan would be required to provide the dollars to purchase oil supplies from Latin America [130].

But American and British viewpoints soon began to differ. Washington instinctively shied away from the use of military force to topple Nasser [*Doc. 28*]. The Americans sought instead a negotiated settlement with Egypt based on international control of the canal.

While Eden continued to present Nasser as a fascist-style dictator to the Americans, September 1956 did witness a brief change in British strategy. The military operation was shelved and Eden entertained the possibility of a 'Suez Canal Users' Association', proposed by American Secretary of State Dulles, as a means of securing the free passage of ships through Egypt. By early October a negotiated settlement between Britain, France and Egypt seemed possible, and the military prepared to suspend operations until the spring of 1957 [152; 185].

But, quite suddenly, force was 'resurrected' by Eden following a secret French diplomatic visit to Britain on 14 October. The French wished to see the end of Nasser, given Egypt's support for Algerian and Tunisian nationalists. The French raised the spectre of an alarming Middle Eastern scenario if the British failed to agree to joint military operations in Egypt: a war might break out between French-supported Israel and Britain's ally, Jordan. Lucas argues that if Eden rejected the French offer, he risked either abandoning Jordan and losing Britain's long-term Middle Eastern position, based on the Iraqi-Jordanian axis, or entering a war with France and Israel [185 *pp. 75–7*].

While vehemently denied by both Eden and his Foreign Secretary, Selwyn Lloyd, after the crisis, two clandestine meetings at Sèvres outside Paris between French, Israeli and British officials finalised an ingenious, yet devious, plan which was kept from the Americans [149]. Israel attacked Egypt first on 29 October. Following an Anglo-French 'ultimatum' to Egypt and Israel, the Anglo-French bombing of Egypt began on 31 October. On 5 November British and French forces entered Egypt on the pretence of separating the Israelis and the Egyptians and, hence, restoring peace in the Middle East [145].

But the outcome of the Suez war hinged on attitudes in Washington. Eden's and Macmillan's assumptions that the Americans would not intervene were quickly shown to be an illusion. The British and the Americans had co-operated effectively in the Middle East prior to Suez; for example, in the Anglo-Egyptian Treaty of 1954, the 1955 Baghdad Pact, and the secret plans for an Egyptian-Israeli peace treaty (plan *Alpha*). Plan *Omega* for the destabilisation of Nasser evinced the American, as well as the British, desire for the Colonel's downfall. But *Omega* 'relied upon subtlety and discretion; an open attack on Egypt would ruin the plan' [153 *p. 27*]. Eisenhower expressed his fears to Eden in September 1956 that an invasion of Egypt would provoke the peoples of the Middle East, and possibly of Africa and Asia generally, into turning away from the West and towards the Russians [*Doc. 28*]. The British were regarded by the Americans as resorting to clumsy, out-of-date methods. 'In 1954 the

British evacuation of Suez signalled a major effort to accommodate Egyptian nationalism. By contrast the 1956 crisis, in American eyes, represented a return to the old imperialism which, it was thought, should have died with the Second World War' [128 *p. 409*].

In line with Arab and independent Commonwealth countries, as well as the Soviet Union, the Americans swiftly condemned, and disassociated themselves from, British, French and Israeli actions. On the night of 1/2 November, the General Assembly of the UN voted sixty-four to five in favour of an American resolution for an immediate cease-fire. The significance of this action for America's leadership of anti-colonial world opinion was not lost on Vice-President Richard Nixon: 'For the first time in history, we have showed independence of Anglo-French policies towards Asia and Africa which seemed to us to reflect the colonial tradition. That declaration of independence has had an electrifying effect throughout the world' [149 *p. 426*]. This is not to say that the Americans occupied the anti-colonial moral high ground. Indeed, rather than conspicuous gunboat diplomacy, the Americans preferred to intervene in Third World affairs through covert methods. An American-backed *coup* had succeeded in restoring the authority of the pro-Western Shah of Iran in 1953, and, as part of *Omega*, the CIA was planning a *coup* against Nasser's supporters in Syria as the Suez invasion began [130; 153].

The Soviet Union also intervened with notes to the British and French governments which raised the spectre of Soviet rocket attacks on London and Paris and Soviet military intervention in the Middle East 'to smash the aggressors and restore peace in the East' [180 *pp. 321–2*]. It remains unclear whether the threat from Moscow was serious. But, given the Soviet decision on 31 October to crush the Hungarian uprising, there was an international sense of panic that the Suez invasion might set off a Third World War [141]. As a result, 'international hostility' toward Anglo-French actions was 'most vividly shown by the willingness of the United States to collaborate with the Soviet Union' to de-escalate Cold War tensions through curtailing the Suez operation [63 *p. xxxiv*]. Above all, however, the Suez crisis exposed the differing aims of Britain and the United States in the Middle East. Eisenhower's number one priority was the exclusion of the Soviets from the region; for Eden the principal concerns were the securing of oil supplies and the upholding of Britain's imperial prestige. As a result, the Americans could afford to be far more pragmatic towards Nasser than the British, especially since the 'canal issue was not a crisis where Soviet influence was manifest' to demand military intervention [139 *p. 211*].

Eden and his Cabinet were ultimately forced into a cease-fire on 6 November by Britain's weak financial position *vis-à-vis* the Americans [146; 148]. 'Far from saving sterling', as Chancellor Macmillan had argued, the invasion 'set off a disastrous run on the pound' [130 *p. 480*]. '[T]he question became not whether, but when, Britain would bow to American imperatives' [148 *p. 216*]. The day after the cease-fire Eden conceded 'we must now get US support' [185 *p. 104*]. The British went cap-in-hand to the Americans. But Washington could in the mid-1950s dictate terms given that the United States government 'not only presided over the main capital markets but funded and controlled international institutions such as the International Monetary Fund (IMF)' [148 *p. 228*]. As Macmillan told his Cabinet colleagues at the end of November 1956, recourse to the IMF would be dependent upon 'the goodwill of the United States Government' and that 'good will could not be obtained without an immediate and unconditional undertaking to withdraw the Anglo-French force from Port Said' [*Doc. 29*]. The frightening possibility of financial collapse forced Eden in December to agree to leave Egypt *unconditionally*. Only then did the Americans save the struggling pound via loans and credits from the IMF and the Export-Import Bank totalling over one billion dollars [148 *p. 231*].

Who is to blame?

The crisis is inexplicable without reference to Eden's character, ill-health and personal loathing of Nasser [185 *pp. 32–5*]. Biographers disagree whether Eden during Suez was courageous, despite his mistakes, or just plain inept [142; 156]. There remains little doubt that 'he made a series of misjudgements fatal for a man in his exposed situation' [149 *p. 557*]. Eden was also haunted by ghosts from his past. Like Churchill, he had built his political reputation during the 1930s in opposition to Neville Chamberlain's policy of appeasement toward the European dictators. Eden had resigned as Foreign Secretary in 1938 over Britain's recognition of fascist Italy's conquest of Ethiopia. The failure of appeasement in the 1930s clearly coloured Eden's thinking in the 1950s. The use of force appeared justified to stop Nasser who was branded a dictator in the mould of Mussolini [13; 16].

However, Suez must also be placed in the wider context of Britain's grand aim of maintaining its sphere of influence in the Middle East and the status and prestige necessary to remain a great power [139; 147; 151]. In addition, other agencies and individuals beyond the prime minister played a role in the events that led to the invasion. MI6, the British intelligence service overseas, had its own plans for toppling Nasser (as well as regimes in Syria and America's client-state Saudi Arabia), and suggested colluding with Israel as early as March 1956. Chancellor of the Exchequer Macmillan was an advocate of war from the outset. He convinced Eden that Washington would not oppose an invasion, and, contrary to the advice of his Treasury officials, he informed the Cabinet that sterling would not be threatened by the conflict [146; 152; 153; 185].

THE CONSEQUENCES

A powerful triumvirate of international factors – the flexing of American financial muscle, condemnation by the UN and the prospect of Soviet intervention – converged at Suez to block Britain's attempt at imperial reassertion. There is no more visible demonstration of how the changed international political and economic environment after 1945 placed severe limits on the exercise of imperial power. Yet, the Suez Crisis has been 'credited with consequences still more dramatic than the episode itself' [187, 2 *p. 29*].

Suez As Watershed

According to Lapping, 'Suez ... is the single most significant initiative by the main imperial powers (Britain and France) that speeded up the end of empire process... . Everybody saw that the imperial gunboat no longer worked' [150 *p. 33*]. After the crisis, Egypt became a centre and inspiration for anti-colonialism while both the Americans and the Soviets began more pro-active campaigns to win the 'hearts and minds' of Africa. In Britain, sweeping defence reforms in 1957, which looked to the development of an independent nuclear deterrent and ended National Service, severely curtailed Britain's ability to suppress colonial insurgents [*Doc. 10*]. After 1959 Prime Minister Macmillan, in partnership with his new like-minded Colonial Secretary, Iain Macleod, forced the pace of decolonisation [150]. Suez was Britain's symbolic 'last stand' in empire; the final stages of decolonisation now went rapidly ahead 'with the outcome conditioned by the demonstration effect at Suez of the harsh limits of British power' [149 *p. 560*]. The leading white settler politician in Kenya, Michael Blundell, was told by a Conservative MP that 'the British cabinet lost its collective nerve after Suez and decided to climb out of any situations which might involve them in critical escapades overseas' [101 *p. 243*].

For Holland, the most telling international aspect of the Suez 'turning-point' 'lay in the US administration's tacit intervention in domestic British politics' [12 *p. 199*]. The Americans now wished to see the back of Eden. The Suez débâcle brought Harold Macmillan to the premiership in January 1957 who, despite his 'hawkish' position over Suez, was widely liked in Washington. From 1957 Macmillan accepted the realities of Britain's shrunken status. He restored the Anglo-American 'special relationship' and played the colonial game to American rules; the inexorable logic of international power politics pointed in the direction of decolonisation [11].

The 'Suez-as-watershed' view is endorsed for different reasons by Lord Beloff. Suez brought about a 'general acceptance in the Conservative party of the fact that the dominance of the United States in world affairs could not be challenged and that the path of safety was at almost any cost to align British policy with that of the United States'. Macmillan was the representative of this 'revolution' in Tory thinking as the party abandoned its role as the 'imperial party'. The Tory vision of a multiracial, British-led Commonwealth as a surrogate for empire had been dashed by the President of India, Nehru, who identified with Egypt, not Britain, during the crisis. Instead, British Conservatives now turned to the possibilities of European unity, 'hitherto of interest only to a minority' [140 *pp. 333–4*].

The aftermath of Suez is central to Louis and Robinson's Anglo-American interpretation of decolonisation: British imperial policy and American Cold War policy symbolically collided at Suez in 1956. 'The Suez crisis ... becomes a touchstone of the inquiry into the nature of post-war imperial power', and shows that ultimately the empire's future hinged on American attitudes. 'Once and for all, it was established that Britain had to work in concert with the United States ... Suez had exposed the American essentials underlying British imperial power for all to see' [130 *pp. 480–1*].

For Cain and Hopkins, meanwhile, it is the dramatic changes in British economic policy after the crisis which require emphasis. The catastrophic run on the pound after the invasion started highlighted 'the contradiction between upholding sterling and funding the military operations needed at times to defend Britain's world role ... This searing experience caused Macmillan to undergo spontaneous conversion: after 1956, the advocate of empire and coercion stood four-square for sterling and peace' [2 *pp. 289-90*]. A series of reviews of Britain's world-wide commitments ensued; the empire-Commonwealth was given up while Europe was taken up.

The Relative Insignificance of Suez

Did American pressure at Suez really force a change of colonial course? Eden's recently released 'Lessons of Suez', circulated to Cabinet colleagues shortly after the crisis, concluded that 'we must review our world position in the light of the Suez experience' and looked forward to a new Britain excelling in technical knowledge; more dependent on nuclear power; pruned of overseas military bases, equipment and troops; and 'working more closely with Europe'. But this did not mean that the empire's days were numbered, and Eden's 'last will and testament' made no reference to accelerating the pace of decolonisation [*Doc. 30*]. Macmillan, on succeeding Eden, did not dissent from Eden's continued imperial vision. Indeed, Macmillan had no blueprint for the colonial future; as he later wrote, was he to be the 'remodeller' or 'liquidator' of empire? [187, 2 *p. 31*]. For the first two years of his premiership, Macmillan persisted with the colonial policies of Colonial Secretary Alan Lennox-Boyd* inherited from Eden. Rather than American pressures during and immediately after Suez, the dramatic change of course between 1959 and 1961 had more to do with considerations arising from unworkable multiracial constitutions in east Africa; African protests against white-settler rule in the Federation of Rhodesia and Nyasaland; the shifts and failings of Belgian and French policy toward Africa; as well as the influence of progressive political opinion in Britain itself [5; 74; 150].

Just as with the loss of India and the Attlee government, there is a case for arguing that colonial policy post-Suez carried on regardless. Suez was a striking event, but there are a number of lacklustre continuities, rather than dramatic discontinuities, which link Eden's administration with that of Macmillan's [187, 2 *p. 29*]. On Britain's economic future it is hard to detect a watershed. As the Governor of the Bank of England astutely recognised, at the time, Suez had merely made the weakness of sterling and the vulnerability of British reserves more widely known. The Treasury and the Bank of England had been aware of the basic problem for some time: the British economy was overextended given the crippling costs of the welfare state and Cold War defence which were now piled on top of the debts incurred during the Second World War. As early as February 1956, the Treasury appreciated that sterling's position in the international economy rested largely on public confidence. It was precisely the Suez operation which had the effect of weakening that confidence. In this sense, Suez simply underlined the importance of pushing onward with existing financial policy: restoring confidence in sterling abroad, initiating an expansion in reserves, and making sterling fully convertible [146 *pp. 177–9*]. These polices had begun in earnest in 1955 before the Egyptian débâcle, and had been Conservative Party policy since 1954.

Suez does not appear to have brought about a sharp U-turn in Britain's economic relations with Europe either. As Ovendale suggests, Harold Macmillan 'only decided' on a turn toward Europe in 1961 following South Africa's exit from the Commonwealth [16 *p. 140*]. Disillusionment with state-induced economic development in the colonies stretched back to the early 1950s, and the July 1957 white paper on development aid 'formalised' more sceptical policies which had dominated since 1954 [187, 2 *p. 30*].

British defence policy also reveals a remarkable degree of continuity pre- and post-Suez. The famous White Paper of 1957 could not have been drawn up entirely between the crisis and its final publication. Rather, it followed on from policy shifts instigated by Eden before Suez. The Conservative's commitment to a British nuclear capacity dated from 1954 while the ending of National Service was a policy determined by the unpopularity of conscription with the electorate and not the consequences of the ill-fated Egyptian invasion [187, 2 *pp. 31–2*].

Nor should Suez be seen as a complete watershed in the nature of Anglo-American relations. As Ovendale points out: 'Britain had been demoted to the status of just one among a number of allies as soon as Eisenhower came into office' [16 *p. 140*]. Moreover, Suez only 'temporarily suspended' joint Anglo-American military and political initiatives. In March 1957 Eisenhower met Macmillan at Bermuda. The conference 'laid the foundations for restored co-operation over Middle Eastern affairs', and recognised that the United States still depended on Britain's material, military and psychological assistance in the Mediterranean, South Asia and the Far East as well [154 *pp. 633, 646*]. The British and the Americans were soon to be co-operating again in 1958 to prevent Jordan and Lebanon falling under the sway of Nasser's United Arab Republic. Later, President Kennedy's administration did not hesitate in offering diplomatic and military assistance for the British intervention of July 1961 in Kuwait to defend the sheikhdom from a possible Iraqi invasion [16; 139].

The 1957 Defence Review did severely limit Britain's ability to act autonomously, and there was an increased reliance on the United States after the Suez crisis. But Britain's aspirations to retain great-power status were not deflected [5; 6]. The failure to crush Nasser did not signpost the end of British power in the Middle East and the Mediterranean. The Libyans had refused to allow the use of the base at Cyrenaica during the crisis. As such, it now appeared of little value [63 *p. xxxiv*]. But, as in the era of Attlee and Bevin, what were regarded as vital military bases, troop deployments and security treaties still 'honeycombed' the region [36 *p. 10*]. In Cyprus, Malta, Jordan, Iraq, Kenya, Aden and the Gulf Sheikdoms, Britain retained considerable interests and influence into the Macmillan administration. The Conservative government was still determined to shape Middle Eastern events, for example, through the construction of a South Arabian Federation, the suppression of rebellions in Muscat and Oman during the late-1950s, and intervention in Kuwait in 1961 [63 *pp. xxxiv–xxxv*; 116; 139] [*Doc. 30*].

The decisive watershed for Britain in the Middle East, it is suggested, was not the Suez disaster in 1956 but the Iraqi Revolution later in 1958 which replaced the pro-British government with a radical regime, reliant on communist support. From then on Britain's interests in the region were clearly limited to the Gulf states, centred on Kuwait with its vast oil deposits [16; 147]. Even then, however, an effective military presence 'East of Suez' was still required in British eyes [5]. This is evinced by plans for building up Kenya and then Aden as the new British stronghold [13; 116]. It was not until January 1968 – following the sterling devaluation of November 1967 – that Wilson's Labour Cabinet reluctantly abandoned Britain's defence commitments in the Middle East as part of the general retreat from 'East of Suez' [*Doc. 16*].

There was no immediate loss of imperial will in tropical Africa either. As late as January 1959 Colonial Secretary Lennox-Boyd believed that independence for Kenya, Tanganyika and Uganda would be delayed until the 1970s. The outcome of Suez neither inspired nationalist leaders nor frightened colonial administrations. Decisions to transfer power in Ghana and Malaya, which both became independent in the course of 1957, were taken before the Suez crisis and could not have been accelerated by it. Low thus suggests that decolonisation was determined by the force of nationalism which was, in turn, conditioned by the unique circumstances pertaining in each individual territory. The process was not affected by international pressures and Cold War exigencies in the wake of Suez [150].

Alternatively, others have argued that the real pressures for rapid colonial change originated from within Britain itself. Tory Cabinet ministers were faced with scant resources to modernise British industry and were extremely reluctant to prune the welfare state, or curtail the consumer boom of the 'you've-never-had-it-so-good' era. The far less politically damaging option was to trim overseas commitments. These concerns 'pre-dated' or were 'unaltered by the failures over Suez' [187, 2 *p. 32*]. As Eden believed, Suez had not so much 'changed our fortunes' as 'revealed realities' [*Doc. 30*].

None the less, it still remains clear that, 'Suez had exposed Britain's inability to act without the approval of the United States' [185 *p. 113*]. This was a lesson not lost on Margaret Thatcher's government during the Falklands Crisis of 1982. Here, the Americans found the Argentinian government 'intractable' and backed Britain. In contrast to Eden at Suez, this enabled Thatcher to 'wind up the politicking ... on cue for the landings' [149 *p. 562*].

7 BRITISH DECOLONISATION IN COMPARATIVE PERSPECTIVE

BRITISH AND OTHER DECOLONISATIONS

The previous chapters have mapped the convergence of metropolitan, colonial and international factors which conditioned the end of the British Empire after 1945, and which varied over time and space. Yet, British decolonisation did not take place within an isolated vacuum; decolonisation was a European phenomenon also encompassing the empires of France, Belgium, Portugal, the Netherlands, Spain and, if we extend our analysis to the very recent past, even that of the Soviet Union/Russia. A non-European power, the United States, also relinquished formal control in its only colony of substance, the Philippines. The British experience of decolonisation shared many of the characteristics with the end of other empires, but it also differed markedly in a number of ways.

SOME COMPARISONS

Imperial Policy: the New Imperialism

Britain was not alone in discovering a new taste for empire for economic and international power-political reasons after the Second World War. The French also 'seized on empire at the very moment it was slipping from their grasp' [158 p. 77]. The franc zone desperately needed to earn and save American dollars as much as the sterling area. In the plan for French domestic reconstruction drawn up in 1949, the expansion of primary production in the empire was given great importance. Economic development in the colonies would contribute to stabilising metropolitan France's balance of payments position, and the economic role of the overseas possessions was to support French industry by providing raw materials and foodstuffs. A new Investment Fund for Social and Economic Development – similar to Britain's system of Colonial Development and Welfare (CD&W) grants – was established in 1946 and endowed with funds to finance development plans in French West and Equatorial Africa. The majority of French development expenditure was channelled into improving colonial transport infrastructure designed to facilitate African exports. A 'second colonial invasion' of French official technocrats and private investors poured into the previously neglected African colonies. Empire would also serve as a source of international political and military strength in a postwar world dominated by the superpowers. France – like Britain – dreamed of being a 'third force' in international affairs [10; 12; 158].

As in the British colonies, French economic and social development was also calculated to stabilise colonial rule through raising living standards and compensating indigenous elites. But, at the same time, it was appreciated in both London and Paris that the resurrection of empire required an element of political reform based on a new 'partnership' of ruler and subject. The Brazzaville Conference of 1944 illustrated that 'a more considered position was to be given the colonial peoples in the imperial system' [158 *p. 61*]. In the African colonies, this entailed the creation of local and regional assemblies which would include Africans, followed by some form of colonial representation in a federal assembly in Paris. The 'spirit of Brazzaville' was fulfilled in 1946 when the new *Union Française* (French Union) abolished colonial status. All the French colonies and protectorates were now to form with metropolitan France 'a union based on free consent'. Morocco, Tunisia and Indochina – the 'Associated States' – would achieve internal autonomy. Control of foreign policy, defence and many economic matters would, however, remain the preserve of Paris. The 'Black' African colonies were set to become 'Overseas Territories' of the new Fourth Republic. Meanwhile, local assemblies provided for a degree of local political autonomy in each of the territories [10; 158].

Shifts in French colonial policy were responses to American critiques as well as nascent nationalism. But the new French Union, like local government reform in the British Empire, was clearly 'intended to fortify' the metropole against international and internal pressures in the future [10 *p. 87*].

The lesser European colonies also hoped to exploit their empires more fully in the postwar world. Belgium's vast estate in central Africa, the Congo, witnessed a massive 'second colonial invasion' in the ten years after the Second World War. Booming Western demand for Congolese exports to the mid-1950s raised the volume of mining production, particularly copper, by 60 per cent. A concomitant wave of immigration increased the white-settler population from about 35,000 in 1946 to 114,000 in 1959.

Although slower to react to demands for political change than the British and French, the Belgian establishment also exhibited signs of a new liberalism designed to stabilise the colonial system. From 1954 reforms in the education system (previously dominated by the interests of the Catholic Church), and a thirty-year plan for decolonisation looked to the promotion of an indigenous middle class of pro-Belgian collaborators. Full citizenship would eventually be attained in a Belgo-Congolese federation. 'The achievement of these ends required an increase in the role of the colonial state and in the finances at its disposal, via increased taxes and borrowing' [174 *p. 266*]. The framework for a new economic and political infrastructure – aimed at modernisation and at preserving the exports from the big European mining combines – was laid out in the first Ten Year Plan for the colony which appeared in 1949, and envisaged expenditure of £183 million [10; 174; 177].

Holland's most important overseas possession was the huge and diverse archipelago known as the Netherlands East Indies which became independent as Indonesia in 1949. The Dutch had long regarded the Netherlands-Indonesia-America triangular trade as vital for metropolitan prosperity. Given the German occupation of the metropolitan Netherlands in 1940, followed by the Japanese invasion of the East Indies in 1942, the restoration of colonial rule in Indonesia was widely regarded as crucial for the revival of the Dutch economy in the postwar world (wrongly as it turned out). 'The future of the Netherlands without the Indies was therefore not even considered except as a state of disaster which had to be prevented' [178 *p. 126*].

To retain these perceived economic benefits, it was also appreciated that political relationships would have to change. After 1946, Holland's 'new imperialism' in Southeast Asia, envisaged the creation of a federal state under the Dutch crown. The Dutch would fight their most intense war ever (in which 170,000 personnel saw military service) not to defend a static prewar colonialism but to instigate their new decolonisation strategy for the Indies [12; 164; 178].

In line with its more democratic West European counterparts, Salazar's authoritarian regime in Portugal was not ready to relinquish control over empire either. In 1951 the colonies were formally declared to be 'overseas provinces' of Portugal, and continued 'to underpin a Lusitanian identity distinct from the messy and dangerous mainstream of European affairs' [165 *p. 83*].

There were economic benefits too: like the British Labour government in its commitment to the sterling area, the Portuguese dictatorship was committed to the integration of the economies of the 'escudo zone'. Colonial currencies were held at parity with the escudo while Portugal's overseas trade deficit was compensated during the 1940s and 1950s by a considerable trade surplus with the colonies in Africa and Asia. The African territories of Angola and Mozambique, in particular, supplied raw materials and offered protected markets for Portuguese industry and fields of investment for Portuguese capital. The 1950s witnessed new development plans devoted to transport, dams and irrigation and which invested funds equivalent to those in British Africa. Funds were earmarked particularly for white immigration schemes [10; 173].

Intensified economic exploitation was accompanied by a modicum of political adaptation: from 1954 it was easier for educated Africans to exercise civil rights, and, although ill-defined, there was talk of an eventual 'Brazilian-style' solution for Africa through the development of self-governing states closely linked to Portugal through the economic and cultural assimilation of indigenous ruling elites (hence, *assimilados*) [10 p. 230]. This was a romantic scenario not unlike Britain's dream of Commonwealth. In the social sphere, the postwar era saw reform of compulsory labour systems in the Portuguese colonies. (Although after 1961 Lisbon backtracked on its reform programme given the determination to defeat the African guerrilla movements, and resources devoted to the promotion of education and social services were far lower than in the decolonising British Empire) [10; 161; 171; 173].

Portugal's fellow Iberian dictatorship in Spain had a much smaller empire in Africa, and after 1945 the Franco regime gave up wartime hopes of taking over the French protectorate in Morocco. None the less, the vast territory of the Spanish Sahara was to prove rich in mineral resources for a relatively poor metropolitan economy – akin to Portugal's – on the margins of Europe [10; 157].

Imperial Policy: 'Disengagement'

As the 1950s wore on, however, Britain was not unique among the European imperial powers in exhibiting signs of economic and strategic 'disengagement' from empire. For France, Marseilles has suggested that there was a deep economic reappraisal of colonies among the economic modernisers who came to the fore during the 1950s. They regarded colonial rule as increasingly inefficient and hoped to transfer resources wasted in empire into modernised and efficient industries capable of holding their own against American, German and Japanese multinationals. As a result, after 1945 the French economy underwent a revolution in technocracy, planning and economies of scale. A more efficient large-scale French capitalism emerged in which the inefficient export industries and antiquated smaller-scale mercantile and commodity capitalism connected with empire had less of a voice. The new super French corporations increasingly looked to economic exchanges with Europe rather than empire. French business pulled out of empire from the early 1950s; a rationalisation which increasingly pointed to decolonisation [170].

Reminiscent again of Britain, economic disengagement coincided with military and strategic reappraisal. Even following defeats at Dien Bien Phu (Vietnam) in 1954 and Suez (alongside Britain) in 1956, the French military generally remained committed to empire and particularly to the war against the Algerian rebels which had begun in 1954. But, during 1958 and 1959, stalemate in Algeria brought the fall of the Fourth Republic, and the return of de Gaulle to French politics as first President of the Fifth Republic. De Gaulle, not unlike Macmillan in Britain following the Suez disaster, had a new vision for the metropole which did not necessarily include colonies. De Gaulle's Algerian policy was increasingly subordinated to a 'primary goal of re-establishing France as a world power' [10 *p. 183*]. This entailed economic modernisation, political reform, and modernisation of the military through a switch from conventional forces to nuclear weaponry.

De Gaulle, although not immediately, intended to make France (with West Germany) leader of Europe from 'the Atlantic to the Urals'; a 'third force' in international power-politics which would be the equal of the superpowers. The Gaullist conception of European France now had little time for outmoded colonialism which, alongside offering few economic benefits, was butchering the military in hopeless guerrilla war. In Algeria, de Gaulle did hope to retain control of nuclear test-sites and valuable oil and gas-fields. But in the eventual settlement of 1962 with the National Liberation Front (FLN), the General was prepared to sacrifice continued control of these interests to liberate France from the 'Algerian drain' on resources [10 *p. 183*; 12].

There were similar indications of Belgian disillusionment with colonial prospects by the later 1950s. The 'spectacular postwar growth' of Congo capitalism had 'slowed' by the mid-1950s, and vast development expenditures placed severe strain on public finances [10 *p. 194*]. There were also signs that the Belgian economy was becoming more and more Europe-centred. These developments coincided with the election of a new Catholic-Liberal coalition in Brussels in 1958, opposed to the domination of the French-speaking establishment which had traditionally monopolised economic and political power in the colonies. At the same time, the Belgian clergy increasingly distanced itself from colonialism, and Belgian politicians could not rely on public opinion to countenance the use of Belgian troops to suppress the Congolese independence movements [10; 174; 177].

Elsewhere in the Low Countries, colonies seemed less attractive economic propositions. Despite the loss of the East Indies, the Dutch economy showed spectacular growth in the 1950s. Marshall Plan aid from America, industrialisation, the EEC, and natural gas strikes in Groningen changed the traditional image of the Netherlands as a resource-poor country, and contributed to a new national self-consciousness in which a continued presence in New Guinea and the Caribbean appeared expensive distractions [12; 178].

Likewise, Iberian economic interests shifted towards Europe through the 1950s and 1960s as greater markets and investments were found there rather than in Africa. By the 1960s, invisible earnings from tourism and from emigrant workers in Germany and France came to dominate Portugal's international exchange position, marginalising the favourable trade balance with the colonies [173 *pp. 220–1*]. The modernising politicians of the centre-left, and the radical armed forces movement, which overthrew the dictatorship in 1974, were representative of this trend. African colonies were no longer seen to benefit metropolitan Portugal; Portugal's diplomatic and economic future lay in the direction of the European community [12; 161; 169; 173].

Given French decolonisation, Spain could not avoid withdrawal from its enclaves in Morocco during the 1960s. The quasi-fascist Franco regime also withdrew from the colonies in west Africa. Expanding trade and tourism links with the rest of Europe pointed Spain away from empire, but Franco's new-found anti-colonialism also served his diplomatic interests in that it might secure support for Spain's claim to the British colony of Gibraltar. (Although Spain did maintain control of the mineral-rich Sahara until 1976.) [10; 157]

Imperial Policy: the Preservation of Post-Colonial Influence

But if the economic and strategic value of colonies was reassessed, it was still hoped that decolonisation would maintain established European commercial and political influence in the developing world. The British hoped to achieve this through the expansion of Commonwealth membership, and the economic and military agreements which generally accompanied the transfers of power. Similarly, independence for Indonesia in 1949 was accompanied by a Netherlands-Indonesian Union, as a new framework for co-operation. As a means of retaining some influence in Southeast Asia and providing a resettlement area for Eurasians and Europeans who felt uncomfortable in the new Republic, the Dutch also retained their presence in New Guinea until 1962 [12; 178].

In the sudden opening up of the political system in the Congo between 1959 and 1960, Belgian decolonisation strategy was designed to allow for post-colonial influence through continued Congolese dependence on Belgian economic, technical and administrative assistance. The proliferation of competing political parties in the Congo would also allow the Belgians an important mediating role [10].

In the war-torn Portuguese Empire, General Spínola, first President of the post-revolutionary Republic, aimed in 1974 to preserve metropolitan interests through a 'Lusitanian Federation' [169].

These Dutch, Belgian and Portuguese schemes came to very little, but the French were more successful in their 'neo-colonial' strategies for preserving post-colonial sway. The French retrieved little from their abrupt exits from Vietnam and Algeria. In Black Africa, de Gaulle's conception in 1958 of a French Community to replace the Union was swiftly superseded by the wholesale granting of independence during 1960. Yet, here, at least, a large measure of French influence was sustained through generous aid packages and preferences for exports within the EEC, co-operative Francophone elites, and military agreements which allowed for the continued stationing of French troops [10; 12].

Colonial Nationalism

However, changing *modus operandi* in the European metropolises can only partly explain the ending of colonial rule. Like the British, the other European imperialists faced the challenge of nationalism in their colonies. Although the nature of nationalist movements varied enormously from territory to territory, they emerged throughout Africa and Asia for broadly similar reasons: growing populations; agricultural depression; migration to the colonial city with consequent unemployment and overcrowding; and the emergence of Western-educated 'national' elites whose aspirations – despite the hopes of colonial planners – could not be accommodated in the postwar colonial order. Popular grievances were articulated and exploited by the elites via mediums largely 'imported' from Europe, such as newspapers, political parties and trade unions which allowed for the 'imagining' of national communities [12; 83; 158]. Colonial disaffection throughout the overseas empires of Europe was often magnified by the dynamics of postwar overrule and the 'second colonial occupation' [111; 114].

Yet, as colonial rule unravelled, nationalist movements often showed themselves to be highly divided. British experiences in territories like India and Nigeria were replicated in other empires as African and Asian elites competed for the spoils of independence. The Indonesian Republican movement involved a bewildering array of nationalist, socialist, communist, youth, military and Islamic groups, and the early years of independence were littered with regional revolts. The South Moluccans, who had developed a 'loyalist' relationship with the Dutch through their conversion to Christianity and their role in the colonial army, sought a separate homeland from 1950; while Muslims in the northern Sumatran state of Aceh desired a new state based on Islamic law [87; 175].

In much of Black Africa, decolonisation represented the competing politics of ethnicity rather than the triumph of mass nationalism as pre-colonial 'primary nations' reinvented themselves [10]. In the Congo, the rapid dissolution of Belgian authority at a local level between 1959 and 1960 accentuated divisions among the Congolese as party organisers appealed to ethnic loyalties. In the southern province of Katanga, separatists were keen to secure the position of local peoples against the encroachments of immigrants, as well as prevent the wealth of the copper mines being siphoned off by Patrice Lumumba's regime at the centre. Supported by the international mining conglomerates, Katanga seceded from the newly-independent state in July 1960. After Lumumba's assassination at the end of 1960, there was no effective central government in the Congo. Only in 1965, following a military *coup*, did the Congo achieve an element of imposed unity and stability [10].

In the former mandate of Ruanda-Urundi, the aftermath of Belgian withdrawal, and the creation of two new states of Rwanda and Burundi in 1962, was no more worthy of praise. The 'acceleration of political activity' in the final stages of decolonisation 'sharpened' ethnic antagonisms between Tutsis and Hutus in both countries, leaving tragic problems for the future [10 *p. 198*].

In Angola, three nationalist groups 'competed with each other as much as they did with the Portuguese' [171 *p. 369*]. All had strong ethnolinguistic and regional bases of support. The rival groups were regularly in conflict, and even within the separate movements splits and fissures emerged. The complexities of the Angolan situation, like that in the Congo after 1960, allowed external actors to exaggerate these divisions after independence in 1975 [10; 19; 160].

International Factors

International pressure was another factor in the process of decolonisation; the British were not alone in facing it. The Dutch exile government in London came under such pressure from the United States to reform its empire that in 1942 Queen Wilhelmina promised a new Dutch Commonwealth after the war. Meanwhile, the insistence of the Americans that their forces be allowed to 'assist' in the defence of Holland's mineral-rich Caribbean territories was regarded as a grave danger to Dutch colonial interests, and ensured that these possessions 'could never return entirely to their pre-war closed colonial worlds' [172 *p. 473*]. In their later military actions to impose a federal state in Indonesia, the Dutch were restrained, firstly, by the mediating role of the UN and secondly, by America's threatened suspension of reconstruction aid and exclusion from NATO. American support for Sukarno's nationalists – because they had suppressed a communist revolt in September 1948 while the Dutch were expending resources vital to the defence of Western Europe against communism in an irrelevant colonial war – was arguably the decisive factor bringing about Indonesian independence in 1949 [12; 168]. The attitude of the United States was again decisive when military confrontation between Indonesia and Holland threatened in 1960 over the continued Dutch occupation of New Guinea. The Dutch government quickly backed down when the Americans indicated their displeasure; in 1962 it was agreed that New Guinea (renamed Irian Jaya) be incorporated into Indonesia [12; 178].

But, as the British also found, the attitude of the United States on decolonisation issues was never clear-cut. As the Cold War arrived in Asia after 1950, the Americans could also boost the threatened empires. The French in Vietnam, just like the British in Malaya, were believed to be fighting international communism [135]. As a result, by 1954 – the year when French forces were symbolically defeated at the highland garrison of Dien Bien Phu – the Americans were shouldering 75 per cent of the cost of France's war against the Vietminh. As a result, the collapse of French resolve (as well as Britain's refusal to be drawn into military conflict) in Indochina greatly frustrated American Secretary of State Dulles. The Americans were thus forced, reluctantly, into negotiation with Britain, Russia and China at the Geneva conference which divided Vietnam into a communist-dominated North and an American-backed South. Neither the Vietminh nor France had much influence on this decolonisation end-game [12; 162].

The Portuguese also found the Americans amenable to their empire. Although President Kennedy had associated the United States with UN denunciations of Portuguese colonialism in the early 1960s, by the end of that decade American economic and military support for the Portuguese empire was covertly stepped up, given fears of communist incursions in the Iberian peninsula as well as in Africa. There was an equally important desire to secure NATO strategic assets in the North Atlantic, especially on the Portuguese Azores [12; 171].

SOME CONTRASTS

Imperial Policy

The British are generally regarded as more liberal in their approach to colonial nationalism than their European counterparts. British administrators did establish a tradition of meeting colonial discontent through reform, allowing for a remarkable degree of foresight compared with the French, Dutch, Belgians and Portuguese. As early as 1839, Lord Durham's report on disturbances in Canada looked forward to internal self-government. Just under a century later, the 1931 Statute of Westminster legally enshrined equality and full independence within the Commonwealth for Australia, Canada, the Irish Free State, New Zealand and South Africa. Here was a model, and an inheritance of procedure, which could be applied to India and the rest of the colonial empire after the Second World War [162].

With the exception of perhaps Portugal and Spain in nineteenth-century Latin America, the other European empires had no such precedents for decolonisation. Even if the results and the pace of decolonisation after 1945 were not anticipated, the British did exhibit a willingness to converse with nationalist leaders. Where wars were fought – for example, in Malaya and Kenya – these were attempts to ensure that independent successor regimes preserved British strategic and commercial interests [162]. A key element in British counter-insurgency strategy, epitomised by General Templer's regime in Malaya after 1952, was the 'political ingredient' whereby moderate nationalists were permitted just enough political space to mobilise the masses as a counter to undesirable radicalism [112].

Decolonisation methods and procedures aside, the French conception of empire was markedly different from Britain's. The French were traditionally 'centralist' rather than 'devolutionist'; the empire was referred to as 'France Overseas' and the ultimate assimilationist aim of French colonial policy was to turn colonial subjects into good French men and women. The Brazzaville Conference of 1944 did initiate some reforms but it made it clear that independence outside the

French bloc was not acceptable. It is illuminating that French development plans for the colonies were drawn up in Paris; the British equivalents were drafted by the colonial government in each particular territory [10].

In other words, the ultimate authority of France over the Union was not a subject for debate. The powers of local assemblies were always circumscribed. Late in the day, the African *loi cadre* or 'Enabling Act' of 1957 introduced universal suffrage and extended the power and responsibilities of colonial assemblies, providing them with a council of ministers. But the governor in each territory was automatically president of the council of ministers and was reserved major powers in the field of security and economics, meaning that 'sovereignty effectively remained in French hands' [158 *p. 122*]. When African nationalists were afforded political space in the 1940s and 1950s it was as colonial representatives within either the French parliament in Paris or the Assembly of the French Union at Versailles, allied to the major French political parties. Britain had long rejected the idea of imperial centralisation in favour of devolution through the Commonwealth [162; 176] [*Doc. 31*].

These attitudes were reinforced by French national *psyche*. Just as defeat at the hands of Germany in 1870 had prompted France's establishment of empire, the German humiliation of the Second World War psychologically underpinned the collective need to reassert empire after 1945. Colonies were believed to be vital in maintaining European France's military, diplomatic and economic great-power standing in the world. The liberation of metropolitan France had been launched from empire, and continued possession of overseas territories gave the French extra bargaining power in a postwar world likely to be dominated by *les anglo-saxons*.

There was a remarkable pro-colonial consensus among the French public which spanned the political spectrum from left to right. Only the communists were prepared to work with the nationalists, and even they discouraged independence in preference for the universal republicanism of the French Union. Indeed, the search for national '*gloire*' through empire served as a means of cementing political and social divisions in metropolitan France. The French military was also far more embedded in empire than Britain's; many a French army officer equated nationalism with Soviet communism which posed a direct strategic threat to France itself [162]. France's refusal to accept the realities of anti-colonialism, in contrast to Britain's more conciliatory attitude, led to larger-scale and bloodier conflicts in the postwar French empire [12; 14; 158; 162].

Empire was an equally central element in national identity in other European countries. 'Injured pride' during wartime, an 'obstinate search for national grandeur' and a deep hostility towards 'traitorous' colonial subjects who had collaborated with the Japanese (alongside misperceived economic value) explains Holland's resort to armed force rather than negotiation to deal with the Indonesian republicans [164; 178 *p. 130*]. Portugal's protracted wars of decolonisation are explicable given that possession of empire was a central tenet of the nationalist dictatorships of Salazar and Caetano (who succeeded the former in 1968). The colonial possessions of mainland Europe were expressions of 'Frenchness'; 'Dutchness' and 'Portugueseness' in ways that the British Empire had never been a central expression of 'Britishness'. The Belgians, meanwhile, with no pretensions to great-power status, contented themselves in their supposedly unique paternalism and saw no need to prepare for decolonisation [10; 177].

The relatively liberal colonialism espoused by British ministers, mandarins and proconsuls permitted greater control over the timing and manner of decolonisation, and to 'play an influential ["neo-colonial"] role in constructing the constitutions, politics and economies of successor states' [162 *pp. 178–9*]. In this sense, the British compared favourably with the Americans who immediately after the war transferred power to the entrenched landholding elite in the Philippines [167]. In return, the Americans were awarded a remarkable set of economic and military privileges in the independent Philippines, and the islands 'continued to have one of the most unreconstructed social orders in Asia' [101 *p. 37*].

The French could manage events to their satisfaction in colonies where there was little unrest; for example, in west Africa. But in Vietnam and Algeria, where there were violent and protracted confrontations, the successor regimes were largely constructed by the nationalists [162]. Likewise, the Dutch federalists could not prevent the Indonesian republicans constructing a unitary state from the numerous islands and diverse communities of the archipelago [12].

Britain's less-committed approach also ensured that co-operation with the other European imperial powers was always problematic and limited. In Africa, for example, there was hardly any common political ground between London and Paris. British constitutional concessions in west Africa from 1948 appeared to the French as a sell-out to selfish nationalism which would ultimately undermine the French Union [63; 166] [*Doc. 31*]. As such, 'Anglo-French collaboration' rarely 'extended beyond fairly minor administrative, technical and economic matters' [63 *p. xlii*]. It was a similar story in Southeast Asia where the more progressive British were keen to distance themselves from French and Dutch colonial wars [46]. Moreover, London's close association with the less liberal imperialists would undermine the 'special relationship' with Washington [63 *p. xlii*].

Britain's domestic political institutions appeared more adaptive to the realities of postwar empire than their European counterparts. Metropolitan Britain is distinguished, from France in particular, by the stability of its political system throughout the decolonisation era: 'from the mid-1940s until the mid-1960s, British imperial policy was characterized by coherence, consistency and strength' [176 *p. 95*]. Britain's political leaders were helped in their decolonisation strategies by a hierarchical two-party system which made it impossible for extremists on either right or left to disrupt policy.

In contrast, the French Fourth Republic lacked the consensual nature of British postwar politics which proved so vital for the successful management of decolonisation [14]. The 'multiplicity of parties and factions' meant that 'no Prime Minister was ever in a position to develop constructive solutions to political problems because of the welter of contradictory commitments made in the course of coalition-making' [12 *p. 165*]. This gave the Algerian *colons* (white settlers), who were represented in the parliamentary system, power to block decolonisation policy [14]. Such a situation never arose in Britain since Kenyan or Rhodesian settlers were not directly represented in Westminster (and these white populations were much smaller anyway). Given a weak executive in the metropole, French colonial officials and military commanders 'on the spot' – who were increasingly disgusted by the 'cowardly' politicians in Paris – were allowed considerable autonomy to act independently in territories like Vietnam and Algeria.

It was the threat of a settler-army *coup* in Algeria against Paris in 1958 that finally dissolved the Fourth Republic and brought de Gaulle to power. Britain never experienced a comparable crisis in its political system induced by the stresses of decolonisation. Lord Salisbury resigned in 1957 over British policy in Cyprus [62], but only the Suez imbroglio of 1956 really intruded into British domestic politics and, even here, the crisis was resolved smoothly by the replacement of Eden with Macmillan and little perceptible change in overall policy. Tory empire-loyalists were easily fobbed off with the Commonwealth ideal as a new focus for overseas 'greatness'.

Alongside France, colonial issues also took their toll on the metropolitan political system in Portugal. The static dictatorship brought about its own downfall through the stubborn continuance of the wars in Guiné, Angola and Mozambique. Primarily, it was the 'maintenance of large conscript armies' which 'placed increasing strains on Portuguese society and its economy' [10 *p. 233*]. In April 1974, the so-called 'Carnation Revolution', led by middle-ranking army officers, installed a military junta under General Spínola. Spínola was a recent veteran of the colonial war in Guiné where he believed the military campaign was being undermined by the absence of any decolonisation strategy for the empire. But Spínola's progressive plans for negotiated peace and the transfer of power within a Lusitanian federation were also superseded as revolutionary pressure in Lisbon forced the general's departure from office at the end of September. This left the socialist leaders of the Armed Forces Movement, many of whom were ideologically disposed towards the African guerrilla vanguard, to engineer the final dénouement of Portuguese imperialism [10; 169; 171].

Colonial Nationalism

Britain's relatively more successful and crisis-free management of decolonisation might also be explained in terms of the quality and character of colonial nationalism it faced. France's opponents, it could be argued, proved far more formidable. In Black Africa the French were fortunate to find elites who were prepared to collaborate with rather than confront them. For example, in the Ivory Coast, under Félix Houphouet-Boigny who had served as a Cabinet minister in Paris, the preferential treatment given in French markets to coffee and cocoa production dictated a policy of prudence among the nationalist elite toward Paris [176].

But in Algeria and Vietnam no such elites existed or emerged. In Algeria the role of the local native elite in the administration and the economy had been pre-empted and usurped by the settlers. As a result, the distress of the Algerian peasantry was directly (and violently) embodied in a guerrilla movement rather than conciliated by a moderate middle class. Once the Algerian revolt began in 1954, the French searched desperately for an authoritative moderate group with whom they could negotiate more favourably than the FLN. They found none simply because the 'class of people who might have seen their future interests tied to France and who might have feared a radical peasant uprising just did not exist in any important number' [176 *p. 110*]. In Vietnam, the French had made the mistake of liquidating (with the help of *Madame Guillotine*) the non-communist nationalists before the war. After the war, France's chosen collaborator, the Emperor Bao Dai, was never able to form a strong enough alliance of moderates to split the union of communism and nationalism in the countryside, as occurred under Tunku Abdul Rahman's Alliance in British Malaya [176].

In Portuguese Africa, from the later 1950s, the character of the liberation movements was very different again, particularly with regard to the strong influence of Marxist analysis among the principal nationalist groupings in Angola, Mozambique and Guiné. The delayed decolonisation of Portuguese Africa produced very different nationalist movements from their 'British' counterparts. They were more explicitly Marxist in ideology, more militant in action and, in the case of Angola, more dependent on external support and influence from the communist bloc [160; 171; 173]. Where the British faced communist-led insurgency – most notably in Malaya – this could be isolated along ethnic, religious and ideological grounds and the communists received little or no outside support.

On the other hand, variation in the nature of colonial politics largely reflected the different character of imperial ideology and sentiment from metropole to metropole. As Low emphasises, given the force of French nationalism expressed through empire, the Vietnamese nationalists, for example, needed to develop a mass political organisation based on a fusion of communist and traditional nationalist thinking led by a highly disciplined elite and backed up by an underground guerrilla force trained in both military and propaganda strategies. But against the less-committed British, Gandhi – and nationalists elsewhere who later followed his example – needed to agitate to gain attention but the non-violent stance allowed the more liberal instincts of British ministers, mandarins, and colonial administrators to prevail [101]. Despite Portugal's self-styled unique multiracial colonialism (Lusotropicalism), the determination of the Salazar regime to hold on to empire, combined with the repressive powers of the Portuguese secret police, pushed elite politicians who had gained an overseas education – like Amil Cabral in Guiné – into much more militant resistance than their forerunners in British Asia and Africa [160; 173].

International Factors

British decolonisers were also fortunate in terms of the international environment they faced. Generally, British statesmen had a better relationship with the Americans than their French contemporaries. During the war, Roosevelt and Churchill did not always see eye-to-eye on colonial matters. But the American President still retained a respect for the British Prime Minister. In contrast, Roosevelt developed a deep loathing for de Gaulle, and the American establishment during the war years, and after, generally suffered from acute Francophobia. At the same time, the leader of the Free French was wary of a possible Anglo-American redrawing of the colonial map, especially given American plans for international trusteeships in French territories such as Morocco and Indo-China and fears of British aggrandisement in the Middle East [158; 176].

The British deeply resented and resisted international interference in their empire, but were, on the whole, more acceptant of American postwar policy than the French [176]. Despite strains in the 'special relationship' during the 1950s (and especially during Suez), by the early 1960s Anglo-American friendship was fully resurrected, epitomised by the close relations of President Kennedy and Prime Minister Macmillan. It is no surprise that de Gaulle increasingly turned his invective against the Anglo-American 'front' [12]. Certainly there was no Franco-American coalition in decolonisation where, perhaps, there was an Anglo-American one [130]. Moreover, as Kahler observes 'in France, political gains could be made on both the Right and the Left by *resisting* the importunity of the North American ally' [14 *p. 365*]. As we have seen, the British followed decolonisation models broadly similar to America's remarkably successful management of political change in the Philippines; the French instinctively rejected such Anglo-Saxon devolution models. Similarly, the French political elite was far less responsive to condemnation of colonial practice from world opinion in the form of the UN and the non-aligned nations such as India [14].

The liquidation of Portugal's empire occurred within an international environment quite different from that which saw the end of the British, as well as the French, Dutch, and Belgian Empires. By the 1970s, the Western Alliance had lost the pre-eminence which it had enjoyed from the mid-1940s to the mid-1960s [171]. This created particular problems in Angola where the MPLA, in its bid to defeat both its Portuguese and nationalist rivals, turned to the Soviet Union and Cuba for military support. The movement nominally took power in the Angolan capital, Luanda, in November 1975. But this only initiated an intensified phase in the civil war between the MPLA and its South African and American-backed rivals [10]. By escaping from empire just a decade earlier, the British avoided the tragic consequences of the globalisation of decolonisation.

The Strange Case of the Soviet Union/Russia

In terms of timescale, the decolonisation of the Soviet Union/Russia is clearly a unique case. Only in December 1991 did the international community which Lenin and Stalin reconstructed from the empire of the Russian Tsars officially expire. This followed the revolutions of

1988–9 which swept away the pro-Soviet communist parties in the Warsaw Pact client states of Eastern Europe. The Soviet empire also differed from the maritime empires of Western Europe in that it was a vast contiguous land mass encompassing numerous ethnic groups within its borders. It prided itself on being a new kind of state in which different peoples were fused together by the common ideology of communism. (Although in reality the Soviet Union, like the Tsarist empire, was based on Russian chauvinism.)

After 1945, the Soviet Union developed an 'informal empire' along its borders in Eastern Europe, maintained by local collaborating Communist Parties. As Clayton suggests, the collapse of a land empire 'raises questions of national identity amounting to angst and loss of self-confidence' not encountered in the old maritime empires of Western Europe [163 *p. 6*]. This goes a long way to explaining the uncompromising Russian military campaign against the republic of Chechnia after December 1994. Russia was able to accept the formal independence of the fourteen non-Russian constituent Republics of the Soviet Union, but loss of territory from *within* the Russian Federation was completely unacceptable. Clayton also points to a number of other contrasts between the ends of the Russo-Soviet and British Empires: the Russians had no superpower ally to oversee decolonisation; the Soviet collapse was the result of economic, political and military 'implosion' at the centre rather than nationalist 'explosion' on the periphery; the break up of the Union was far speedier than the British Empire's staged transition into Commonwealth, leaving far greater problems of administrative inexperience and economic dependency in the new successor states [163].

Even so, there remain broad parallels in the collapse of the Soviet Union with the British experience some thirty to forty years earlier. Most notably, the impetus for change originated at the imperial centre. Not unlike Clement Attlee in 1945 Britain, Mikhail Gorbachev in 1985 wished to use the resources of the periphery to rejuvenate the economically stagnant and militarily backward Soviet system. A central tenet of the reform programme known as *perestroika* was the elimination of corruption at a local level. But the weeding out of corrupt local officials in territories such as Georgia, Uzbekistan and Kazakhstan was regarded as an unwarranted intrusion of the centre into the affairs of 'colonial' peoples which threatened local traditions. This Soviet 'second colonial occupation' was resented, not least, because many local officials were replaced by Russians; *perestroika* was increasingly seen to be in the interests of Russia alone. Combined with economic stagnation and terrible housing conditions in many of the Republics, resentment turned into riots and rebellions directed against the imperial centre [159].

At the same time, Gorbachev furnished nationalists with platforms for action. Popular Fronts in all the Republics were encouraged by the Soviet government in an attempt to build up mass support for economic reform. As with local government reform in British Africa after 1945, this process of democratisation spiralled out of the control of the imperial presidium. Epitomised by *Saiudis* in the Baltic Republic of Lithuania, the Popular Fronts became increasingly independent of Soviet power; democracy became equated with national self-determination; and the local Communist Parties were increasingly regarded as organs of Russian domination. The Popular Fronts trounced the officially recognised Communist Parties throughout the Soviet empire in the local elections of 1989. These victories were swiftly followed by declarations of sovereignty and independence which overran the entire union during 1990 and 1991 [159]. As the British found, once the lid was off the colonial bottle the nationalist outpourings were almost impossible to contain. Yet, historians must also bear in mind that what often strained the transfer of power was inter-ethnic tension and competing nationalisms. For example, the struggle of Armenians and Azeris over the disputed territory of Nagorno-Karabakh has been compared with the communal conflicts which ultimately paralysed imperial rule in British India [163]. The end of the Russo-Soviet Empire was as much a struggle within and between the Republics as a struggle with Moscow; this was why the Kremlin, just like Whitehall, often lost control of the decolonisation process [159; 163].

A final comparison between the end of British and Russian imperialism is also instructive. The Russians, like the British before them, have attempted to maintain influence in their former dependencies despite formal, 'flag' independence. The president of Russia, Boris Yeltsin, after helping to abolish the Soviet Empire in 1991 immediately latched on to the concept of the Commonwealth of Independent States (CIS) – an idea clearly modelled on the British Commonwealth. Russia's intended CIS army has not emerged, but this new diplomatic subsystem has allowed for a modicum of continued co-ordination of defence facilities and co-operation on economic matters in the post-imperial world [163].

Indeed for all European, and non-European, decolonisers, the end of colonial rule was never predicated on the principle of abandonment of influence. After a brief epoch of formal rule, Britain and other imperial powers *attempted* to revert to the age-old pursuit of 'informal empire' [8; 90; 130].

PART SIX: DOCUMENTS

DOCUMENT 1   'A FINANCIAL DUNKIRK'

Lord Keynes was an economic adviser to the Treasury during the Second World War. In this memorandum for the postwar Labour Cabinet he dramatically exposed the weakness of the British economy at the end of the war: the British war effort had been dependent on massive loans from the United States and the liquidation of overseas assets. As a result, Britain was overspending its own income by over £2,000 million a year. To avoid economic disaster, drastic measures were called for. After Cabinet discussion of the memorandum, Keynes was dispatched to Washington where he eventually negotiated a $3.75 billion loan.

27. It seems ... that there are three essential conditions without which we can have not a hope of escaping what might be described, without exaggeration and without implying that we should not eventually recover from it, a financial Dunkirk. These conditions are (a) an intense concentration on the expansion of exports, (b) drastic and immediate economies in our overseas expenditure, and (c) substantial aid from the United States on terms which we can accept. They can only be fulfilled by a combination of the greatest enterprise, ruthlessness and tact.

28. What does one mean in this context by a "financial Dunkirk"? What would happen in the event of insufficient success? That is not easily foreseen. Abroad it would require a sudden and humiliating withdrawal from our onerous responsibilities with great loss of prestige and acceptance for the time being of the position of a second-class Power, rather like the present position of France. From the Dominions and elsewhere we should seek what charity we could obtain. At home a greater degree of austerity would be necessary than we have experienced at any time during the war. And there would have to be an indefinite postponement of the realisation of the best hopes of the new Government. ...

Cabinet memorandum by Lord Keynes, 13 August 1945, [184, 2], p. 4.

DOCUMENT 2   THE NEW ECONOMIC IMPERIALISM

Britain's precarious balance of payments position underlined the economic significance of the colonial empire. Here Sir Stafford Cripps, the Minister for Economic Affairs, hammers home the new importance of Africa to an audience of colonial governors.

Our own set-back in production consequent upon war devastation and our inability to buy foodstuffs and raw materials from the sterling area or non-dollar countries, coupled to the need of other sterling countries to buy manufactured goods from the USA, has resulted in the very heavy adverse balance of dollars running at the rate of between £600 and £700 millions a year for the sterling area. ...

It is the urgency of the present situation and the need for the Sterling Group and Western Europe both of them to maintain their economic independence that makes it so essential that we should increase out of all recognition the tempo of African economic development. We must be prepared to change our outlook and our habits of colonial development so that within the next 2-5 years we can get a really marked increase of production in coal, minerals, timber, raw materials of all kinds and foodstuffs and anything else that will save dollars or will sell in a dollar market. ...

Speech by Cripps to the African Governors' Conference, 12 November 1947, [184, 1], pp. 299, 300.

DOCUMENT 3   BRITAIN AS A GREAT POWER IN THE POSTWAR WORLD

Labour's Foreign Secretary, Ernest Bevin, was determined that Britain must remain a great power. With the expansion of Soviet influence in Eastern Europe, Bevin proposed a British-led Western Union.

... [W]e should seek to form with the backing of the Americas and the Dominions a Western democratic system comprising, if possible, Scandinavia, the Low Countries, France, Portugal, Italy and Greece. ... [W]e should of course wish also to include Spain and Germany, without whom no Western system can be complete ...

Provided we can organise a Western European system ... backed by the power and resources of the Commonwealth and of the Americas, it should be possible to develop our own power and influence to equal that of the United States of America and the U.S.S.R. We have the material resources in the Colonial Empire, if we develop them, and by giving a spiritual lead now we should be able to carry out our task in a way which will show clearly that we are not subservient to the United States of America or to the Soviet Union.

Cabinet memorandum by Ernest Bevin, 4 January 1948, [184, 2], pp. 317, 318.

DOCUMENT 4   POLITICAL DEVELOPMENT IN AFRICA

In September 1946 Andrew Cohen, head of the Africa Division in the Colonial Office, proposed a radical new policy of local government reform in Africa designed eventually to transfer power to Africans. One of Cohen's senior colleagues, Frederick Pedler, outlined why the new policy was urgently required.

2. Africa is now the core of our colonial position; the only continental space from which we can still hope to draw reserves of economic and military strength. Our position there depends on our standing with Africans in the mass. And this depend [s] on whether we make a success of African *local* government. ...

8. What is wanted now is a vigorous policy of African local government which will progressively democratise the present forms and bring literates and illiterates together, in balanced and studied proportions, for the management of local finances and services. Failing this we shall find the masses apt to follow the leadership of demagogues who want to turn us right out very quickly. ...

Minute by Pedler, 1 November 1946, [184, 1], pp. 117–18.

DOCUMENT 5   THE OFFICIAL AIM OF BRITISH COLONIAL POLICY

For the Colonial Office, the eventual transfer of power in the colonial empire and, hence, the expansion of Commonwealth membership, could have great advantages for the United Kingdom. British and colonial interests would be prejudiced, however, by any premature withdrawal.

There is no ambiguity in the official statement of our colonial policy. The central purpose ... "is to guide the colonial territories to responsible self-government within the Commonwealth in conditions that ensure to the people both a fair standard of living and freedom from oppression from any quarter." ...

3. But there is no intention to abandon responsibilities prematurely. Self-government must be effective and democratic self-government. No colonial territory will be expected to fend for itself until it is in a position to do so, and to build up and maintain a satisfactory standard of living. Nor will responsibility be relinquished without satisfactory assurances for the liberty and well-being of the individual; it is intended that government shall be based on representative institutions. ...

7. We also aim, in our colonial policy, at strengthening the Common-wealth. We believe that when our colonies achieve self-government most, if not all, will choose to follow the recent example of Ceylon and remain in the Commonwealth as full and equal partners. In this way there will be an ever-widening circle of democratic nations exerting a powerful stabilising influ-ence in the world.

Colonial Office International Relations Department Paper, May 1950, [184, 1], pp. 334–5.

DOCUMENT 6   **WITHDRAWAL FROM INDIA**

As early as December 1946 the Cabinet appreciated that the British military and administration could not be expected to function in the event of civil war in India.

... *The Prime Minister* [Clement Attlee] said that it was impossible to be con-fident that the main political Parties in India had any real will to reach agree-ment between themselves. Pandit Nehru's [President of the Indian National Congress] present policy seemed to be to secure complete domination by Congress throughout the government of India. If a constitution was framed which had this effect, there would certainly be strong reactions from the Mus-lims. Provinces with a Muslim majority might refuse to join a central Govern-ment on such terms at all; and the ultimate result of Congress policy might be the establishment of that Pakistan which they so much disliked. The Prime Minister warned the Cabinet that the situation might so develop as to result in civil war in India, with all the bloodshed which that would entail. ...

The Cabinet felt that ... [t]he strength of British forces in India was not great. And the Indian Army, though the Commander-in-Chief had great influ-ence with it, could not fairly be expected to prove a reliable instrument for maintaining public order in conditions tantamount to civil war. One thing was quite certain viz., that we could not put back the clock and introduce a period of firm British rule. Neither the military nor the administrative machine in India was any longer capable of this.

Cabinet conclusions (confidential annex), 10 December 1946, [186, 9], p. 319.

DOCUMENT 7   **WITHDRAWAL FROM PALESTINE**

A similar situation to India confronted the British in Palestine by the autumn of 1947 given the competing claims of the Arab and Jewish communities.

21. ... our withdrawal from Palestine, even if it had to be effected at the cost of a period of bloodshed and chaos in the country, would have two major

advantages. British lives would not be lost, nor British resources expended, in suppressing one Palestinian community for the advantage of the other. And ... we should not be pursuing a policy destructive of our own interests in the Middle East ...

Cabinet memorandum by Bevin, 18 September 1947, [184, 1], p. 75.

DOCUMENT 8 **TREASURY DISENCHANTMENT WITH COLONIAL DEVELOPMENT**

As early as 1952 Treasury enthusiasm for economic development in the colonies was waning.

2. ... [I]t seems to me that the whole conception of Commonwealth development as the solution to our difficulties is becoming something of a castle in the air. We know all the difficulties of raising funds from the UK or from private American sources. We have a shrewd suspicion that US Government aid won't go anywhere near to filling the gap. We haven't very much faith in the capacity of the new Dominions to pull themselves up by their bootstrings. And now we have evidence that, even if the money were forthcoming, there are very few winners in the Colonial Empire.

3. It really looks as if our only effective cards are: –

(a) Pushing ahead with the slow business of basic development which is quite unremunerative in the short run;

and

(b) hoping that the American mining companies will find new deposits to exploit in the sterling area.

... [I]t does suggest that the flood of weekend speeches on the boundless possibilities of developing the Empire may be giving rise to quite exaggerated hopes ...

Letter from Flett, Treasury to Melville, Colonial Office, 30 June 1952, [187, 2], pp. 176–7.

DOCUMENT 9 **THE ECONOMIC ATTRACTIONS OF EUROPE**

By the mid-1950s certain Conservative cabinet ministers were arguing for a closer economic association with Europe. In a Cabinet discussion in September 1956 Peter Thorneycroft, the President of the Board of Trade, supported a proposed European Free Trade Area.

Association with Europe ... would provide United Kingdom industry with a unified market of the size which modern technical developments demanded.

The proposals for achieving this would place the United Kingdom for the first time in a combination equal in scale to the other two great trading units of the world, *viz.*, the United States and the Soviet Union. This step would reverse the trend towards the Balkanisation of markets and the fragmentation of economic power in Europe ... It must be recognised that, as a member of such an association, United Kingdom industry would be confronted with more intense competition from Europe in the home market. At times of disequilibrium the Government would need to be prompt and effective in applying remedial measures. But these prospects could not be avoided by remaining aloof from the proposed federation; and our economy would not survive for long if our industries could not compete on level terms with Europe ... As British exporters could not, in any event, escape a competitive struggle with European industry, it would be contrary to our interests to reject the advantages offered by a unified mass market.

Cabinet conclusions, 14 September 1956, [182, 3], pp. 125–6.

DOCUMENT 10   **SHIFTS IN DEFENCE POLICY**

The Macmillan government's defence white paper of April 1957 was the culmination of a number of reviews during the 1950s.

7. Over the last five years, defence has on average absorbed ten per cent of Britain's gross national product. Some seven per cent of the working population are either in the Services or supporting them ... In addition, the retention of such large forces abroad gives rise to heavy charges which place a severe strain upon the balance of payments ...
12. It must be frankly recognised that there is at present no means of providing adequate protection for the people of this country against the consequences of an attack with nuclear weapons ...
15. The free world is to-day mainly dependent for its protection upon the nuclear capacity of the United States. While Britain cannot by comparison make more than a modest contribution, there is a wide measure of agreement that she must possess an appreciable element of nuclear deterrent power of her own. British atomic bombs are already steady in production, and the Royal Air Force holds a substantial number of them. A British megaton weapon has now been developed. This will shortly be tested and thereafter a stock will be manufactured.
16. The means of delivering these weapons is provided by medium bombers of the V-class. ... It is the intention that these should be supplemented by ballistic rockets. Agreement has recently been reached with the United States Government for the supply of some medium-range missiles of this type ...
40. ... the Government are satisfied that Britain could discharge her overseas responsibilities and make an effective contribution to the defence of the free world with armed forces much smaller than at present ...

43. National Service inevitably involves an uneconomic use of manpower, especially in the training organisation. There are at present no less than 150,000 men training or being trained in the establishments of the three Services. This high figure is due, in large measure, to the continuous turnover inseparable from National Service, the abolition of which would make possible substantial savings in manpower ...

46. In the light of the need to maintain a balanced distribution of the national resources the Government have made a comprehensive review of the demands of defence upon the economy and of the country's military responsibilities. They have concluded that it would be right to aim at stabilising the armed forces on an all-regular footing at a strength of about 375,000 by the end of 1962 ...

47. The Government have accordingly decided to plan on the basis that there will be no further call-up under the National Service Acts after the end of 1960.

Defence: Outline of Future Policy, Cmd 124, HMSO, April 1957.

DOCUMENT 11   THE CONTINUED IMPORTANCE OF THE STERLING AREA

In 1957 an influential panel of experts, headed by Lord Radcliffe, was appointed by the Chancellor of the Exchequer to enquire into the working of the monetary and credit system.

657. Although there have been occasions when the functioning of the sterling area has thrown an added strain on the reserves and when the capital requirements of the area have added to the total load on the reserves of the United Kingdom, we are satisfied that it is in the interest of this country to maintain existing arrangements. We do not think it possible to dissociate these arrangements either from the long-standing trading relationships that lie behind them or from the political and other links by which most of the members are joined in the Commonwealth. What is decisive, in our view, is the general harmony of interest between the United Kingdom economy and that of the rest of the sterling area, and the mutual convenience of free multilateral trading relationships within the area.

Report of the Committee on the Working of the Monetary System, Cmd. 827, HMSO, 1959, pp. 240–1 cited in [6; 19].

DOCUMENT 12   THE ADVANTAGES OF THE
COMMONWEALTH

The Committee on Commonwealth Membership reported in 1954 on the
advantages for the UK of expanding Commonwealth membership to former
colonial territories likely to be independent in the 'next ten or twenty years'
(for example, the Gold Coast, Nigeria and Malaya).

6. What purposes will be served if all the countries in this group are held
together in the political association of the Commonwealth? What advantages
shall we gain?

(i) We shall support and strengthen the political influence of the United
Kingdom throughout the world. In former days the influence exercised by our
small country of fifty million people was greatly enhanced by our possession
of overseas dependencies in every part of the world. ... If we are to maintain
our influence as a world power we must increasingly rely on our position as
primus inter pares in a group of independent Commonwealth countries. ...

(ii) We shall strengthen the economic position of the United Kingdom by
adding political cohesion to the sterling area.

(iii) We shall maintain such benefits to Commonwealth trade as can still be
secured through the system of Imperial Preference.

(iv) We shall strengthen our defence potential.

... We cannot attain our defence objectives except as leaders of all the
Commonwealth countries, independent and dependent. There are great
uncertainties in this. Thus, we cannot count on having the support of India's
military manpower, as we could before 1947 ... But we can hope that by wise
political leadership we may be able to mobilise a considerable part of the
Commonwealth's military resources in support of some causes, at any rate. ...
Meanwhile, the political connection between the independent countries of the
Commonwealth gives us valuable facilities, in communications, raw materials
and industrial potential, to support such Commonwealth forces as may be
engaged in a future war.

(v) Countries which maintain the British connection are less likely, in the
period of their political immaturity, to pass under the influence of hostile
Powers. ... [T]here is still a risk that some of the territories now nearing the
stage of independence (*e.g.*, a Malayan Federation) might, if they chose independence outside the Commonwealth, fall under the influence of a hostile
Power – whether by way of internal penetration or by open aggression. This
risk will be reduced if they remain within the political association of the Commonwealth.

(vi) The Commonwealth is as yet the only effective international organisation which links together in an intimate association both European and non-
European peoples. As such it now provides a valuable bridge between the
West and Asia, and in the coming generation it could the same with Africa. To
play this rôle, the Commonwealth must retain its multi-racial character with
equality between member nations of different races.

(vii) From a broader point of view we may have faith that countries which have inherited, whether by blood or by upbringing, the British traditions and outlook on life will be more likely to work for peace and to exercise a healthy influence in international affairs. They will be able to do so more effectively if they are linked together in a single political association.

'The Future of Commonwealth Membership', Report by the Official Committee, 21 January 1954 [187, 2], pp. 287–8.

DOCUMENT 13   MANAGING NATIONALISM

By the 1950s a central tenet of British colonial policy was to bolster moderate nationalists – often through co-option into government – as a means of preserving British economic and strategic interests in post-colonial regimes. By the summer of 1955 both Singapore and the Federation of Malaya had achieved a large measure of internal self-government. Malcolm MacDonald, the British Commissioner General in Southeast Asia, urged an audience of business leaders to support, rather than obstruct, the orderly transfer of power as a check to 'violent Communism'.

This is a revolutionary time in Asia. Right across the continent an upsurge of Nationalist feeling, like a tidal wave, has been sweeping away foreign colonial governments, whether those governments were good, bad or indifferent. ... It was inevitable, it was natural that the great desire for national freedom which is inspiring the whole of Asia should communicate itself to, should infect the peoples of Malaya and Singapore. And it is right that the Governments of Singapore and the Federation should demand with considerable insistence first self-government in their internal affairs, and afterwards, at a later date, independence. If the Governments did not advocate them, the support of the people would pass to the forces of violence, of destruction and of chaos in these territories. We should be glad that the Labour Front [in Singapore], the alliance in the Federation and other democratic, constitutional parties there are making themselves the champions of these legitimate aspirations of the people, because that is the best assurance that the process of change in Malaya shall continue to be peaceful and constitutional as well as radical, causing the least possible upset to the economy and security of the country. ...

Speech by Malcolm MacDonald at the Rotary Club, Singapore, 24 August 1955, Inchcape Archives, Guildhall Library, Borneo Company Ltd., Ms. 27259/2, Enclosure in A. Tanner, deputy general manager, Malaya, Borneo Company Ltd to A. R. Malcolm, managing director, London, Borneo Company Ltd, 27 August 1955.

DOCUMENT 14   NO SHABBY RETREAT

In an address to British officials in Singapore in early 1958, Prime Minister Harold Macmillan was keen to stress that decolonisation was not a sign of weakness.

... [T]here was no reason why we should be ashamed of our post-war record. In India the transfer of power had been made in such a way as to create friendship where otherwise there might have been enmity and bitterness. During his recent visits to India, Pakistan and Ceylon he had been greatly impressed by the friendship and strength of common purpose which still bound those countries to the rest of the Commonwealth. Throughout these countries, though we no longer had authority, we still had great influence. ... the Commonwealth was not breaking up; it was growing up. The Commonwealth as a whole still had great influence in the world, and there was no reason why that influence should not increase. And the United Kingdom itself had great opportunities to influence world affairs through the medium of the Commonwealth association. The material strength of the old Commonwealth members, if joined with the moral influence of the Asiatic members, meant that a united Commonwealth would always have a very powerful voice in world affairs. ...

... Now, once again, having lost our pre-eminence in material strength, we had to learn to exert our influence in other ways. Once more we should be living by our wits, as we had in earlier periods of our history. ...

PREM 11/2219, Record of the Final Session of the Annual Conference of the Commissioner-General, Southeast Asia, 19 January 1958. Note by Brook, 20 January 1958 cited in [69].

DOCUMENT 15   THE LABOUR PARTY AND 'SETTLER' AFRICA IN THE 1960S

From 1956 the Labour opposition distanced itself from Conservative colonial policy by supporting eventual black-majority rule in 'Settler' Africa based upon the principle of 'one man, one vote'. None the less, Labour politicians still had grand imperial visions for Africa: in July 1961 Labour's spokesman on colonial affairs, James Callaghan, looked forward to the creation of a huge, pro-British African Dominion linking together the Central African Federation with the territories of East Africa.

... I was delighted to see the successful outcome of the talks between Uganda, Kenya and Tanganyika about the future of the East African High Commission. ... What these three great Territories, comprising between 25 million and 30 million people, have decided is that they will come together, that theirs shall be a rudimentary assembly to be established with legislative powers, that there will be common services maintained through a special organisation and that there will be the beginnings of a merging of these three Territories. I am sure that anything that can be done towards that end will ... assist the economic development of these territories ...

I believe that, looking ahead, there is no reason why we should limit our vision, whether it be a matter of practical politics or not, to a Central African Federation [Southern Rhodesia, Northern Rhodesia and Nyasaland] torn by dissension and disagreement yet rich in many of the material resources, such as minerals and tobacco, on the one hand, and an East African Federation, with a population three times as great as that of Central Africa, on the other. ... I do not know why these Territories should necessarily expect to remain separate. I am looking some years ahead, but if we look at the geography there is no reason why they should not come together. The combined area of these six countries will be very little larger than that of the Sudan or the Congo or Algeria. It will be far smaller than territories like India. There seems to be no reason at all why we should erect or expect to erect a series of little States in this part of Africa, all of them working separately.

... [T]here seems to be no reason why the six Territories should not at some time see their future together, and I believe they could have a harmonious future. They have many things in common. They have a language in common over a wide area. They have economies which are complementary to each other. They have social and educational institutions of a similar nature.

... [W]e are founding something which could grow and bring peace, solace and a proper form of development to everyone in these Territories, from Bechuanaland in the South to the tip of Tanganyika in the North. It would be a unit which would be quite possible.

Speech by James Callaghan in the House of Commons, 25 July 1961, Parliamentary Debates (Hansard), House of Commons, Official Report, 5th Series, vol. 645, col. 253–5, cited in [6], p. 29.

DOCUMENT 16   WITHDRAWAL FROM EAST OF SUEZ

The decision to withdraw Britain's considerable military contingents from the bases 'East of Suez' in January 1968 has been described as a 'firm date to mark the end of the British empire' [17 p. 343]. The decision followed the great sterling crisis of 1967.

11. ... There is no military strength whether for Britain or for our alliances except on the basis of economic strength; and it is on this basis that we best ensure the security of the country. We therefore intend to make to the alliances of which we are members a contribution related to our economic capability while recognising that our security lies fundamentally in Europe and must be based on the North Atlantic Alliance ...

12. We have accordingly decided to accelerate the withdrawal of our forces from their stations in the Far East ... and to withdraw them by the end of 1971. We have also decided to withdraw our forces from the Persian Gulf by the same date. The broad effect is that, apart from our remaining dependencies and certain other necessary exceptions we shall by that date not be maintaining military bases outside Europe and the Mediterranean.

Speech by Prime Minister Harold Wilson to the House of Commons, 16 January 1968, [183], p. 165.

DOCUMENT 17   NEO-COLONIALISM IN KENYA

In September 1964 the new Prime Minister of independent Kenya, Jomo Kenyatta, made a major speech to an audience of business leaders in Kenya's capital Nairobi. Although he envisaged a greater role for the state in establishing a mixed economy, expatriate investments would be safe under 'African Socialism'.

We consider that nationalization will not serve to advance the cause of African Socialism.

You will appreciate that we have gone to greater pains to guarantee private investment than most countries have done. The Constitution provides safeguards for private property. In addition to these, the Government has provided further safeguards in the proposed Foreign Investments (Protection) Bill. Our taxation system, including investment allowances, offers further testimony of our determination to assist. I urge you, therefore, to study this Act, and reassure your associates overseas that it is the Government's intention, not only to continue to work together with private enterprise, but also to promote conditions in which private enterprise can thrive. In this connection, Government will continue the policy of tariff protection for pioneer and infant industries, including refunds of custom duty for imported raw materials.

Speech by Jomo Kenyatta, 29 September 1964 in Jomo Kenyatta, *Harambee! The Prime Minister of Kenya's Speeches, 1963–1964*, Oxford University Press, 1964, p. 79.

DOCUMENT 18   THE ROOTS OF ANTI-COLONIAL
VIOLENCE IN KENYA

A Kenyan guerrilla leader explains how wartime and immediate postwar experiences led him to adopt violent struggle against colonialism in the 1950s. The Mau Mau forest fighters were united by secret oaths.

Late in 1941 I decided to go into the army ... We were drafted to Ceylon ... After completing some rigorous training manoeuvres in Ceylon we left on 12

July 1943 by ship, rail and road for the Burma Front. ...
In 1944 we returned to India from the Kalewa battlefront. I took back
with me many lasting memories. Among the shells and the bullets there had
been no pride, no air of superiority from the European comrades-in-arms. We
drank the same tea, used the same water and lavatories, and shared the same
jokes. There were no racial insults, no references to 'niggers', 'baboons' arfd
so on ...
I had learnt much, too, about military organization. ...
Perhaps most important, I had become conscious of myself as a Kenya
African, one among millions whose destinies were still in the hands of foreigners, yet also one who could see the need and the possibility of changing
that situation. ...
In 1946, I had joined the Kenya African Union ... Although many of us
had great hopes for this organization, past experience had taught us that it
might well not be enough. Still it was the only public and national political
organization we had. I was also a member of the Transport and Allied Workers'
Union ... At that time the trade unions had the most militant leaders and were
the most active groups working for Independence in the City [Nairobi]. ...
In late 1950 an old Army friend of mine, Kamau, asked me to visit him at
Naivasha. ... Kamau and I found we were at one in thinking that something
decisive must be done soon to show the Government that the people were
growing angry. Kamau asked me to go with him to some other friends, also
living on the farm, and I gladly went. It was thus in Naivasha that I took for
the first time the oath of unity and dedication in the struggle for the freedom
of my country. ...
During the next two years I was a fireman on the Railways by day and a
revolutionary by night. I rapidly became a trusted confidant of the Nyeri
Committee and organized and guarded the oath ceremonies which were daily
being stepped up. ...

Waruhiu Itote, *'Mau Mau' General* reproduced in [180], pp. 316–17.

DOCUMENT 19   THE GOLD COAST DISTURBANCES 1948

*A British Commission of Enquiry summarises the causes of the boycotts,
strikes and riots which challenged the colonial regime in the Gold Coast in
early 1948.*

... In the main, the underlying causes may be divided into three broad catego-
ries: political, economic and social. ...

A. Political
(i) The large number of African soldiers returning from service with the
Forces, where they had lived under different and better conditions, made for a
general communicable state of unrest. Such Africans by reason of their con-

tacts with other peoples including Europeans had developed a political and national consciousness. The fact that they were disappointed with conditions on their return, either from specious promises made before demobilisation or a general expectancy of a golden age for heroes, made them the natural focal point for any general movement against authority.

(ii) A feeling of political frustration among the educated Africans who saw no prospect of ever experiencing political power under existing conditions and who regarded the 1946 Constitution as mere window-dressing designed to cover, but not to advance their natural aspirations.

(iii) A failure of the Government to realise that, with the spread of liberal ideas, increasing literacy and a closer contact with political developments in other parts of the world, the star of rule through the Chiefs was on the wane. The achievement of self-government in India, Burma and Ceylon had not passed unnoticed on the Gold Coast.

(iv) A universal feeling that Africanisation was merely a promise and not a driving force in Government policy, coupled with the suspicion that education had been slowed up and directed in such a way as to impede Africanisation. ...

B. Economic

(i) The announcement of the Government that it would remain neutral in the dispute which had arisen between the traders and the people of the Gold Coast over high prices of imported goods and which led to the organised boycott of January-February 1948.

(ii) The continuance of wartime control of imports, and the shortage and high prices of consumer goods which were widely attributed to the machinations of European importers.

(iii) The alleged unfair allocation and distribution of goods in short supply, by the importing firms.

(iv) The Government's acceptance of the scientists' finding that the only cure for Swollen Shoot disease of cocoa was to cut out diseased trees, and their adoption of that policy combined with allegations of improper methods of carrying it out.

(v) The degree of control in the Cocoa Marketing Board which limited the powers of the farmer's representatives to control the vast reserves which are accumulating under the Board's policy.

(vi) The feeling that the Government had not formulated any plans for the future of industry and agriculture and that, indeed, it was lukewarm about any development apart from production for export.

C. Social

(i) The alleged slow development of educational facilities in spite of a growing demand, and the almost complete failure to provide any technical or vocational training.

(ii) The shortage of housing, particularly in the towns, and the low standards of houses for Africans as compared with those provided for Europeans.

(iii) The fear of wholesale alienation of tribal lands leaving a landless peasantry. ...

Report of the Commission of Enquiry into Disturbances in the Gold Coast, 1948, [180], pp. 312–14.

DOCUMENT 20 THE 'SECOND COLONIAL OCCUPATION' IN CENTRAL AFRICA

The unpopularity of agricultural improvement measures introduced by colonial governments in Africa was often capitalised upon by nationalist leaders. Ecological problems in the central African countryside were a result of pressures on land use, intensified by the postwar influx of white settlers.

(a)

38. About ten years ago the Government enacted legislation under which rules were made to prevent soil erosion. One of these rules is that sloping land should not be cultivated unless ridges or bunds have been erected along the contour; this means a good deal of labour just before the rains come and when the ground is dry and hard. Another rule is that gardens must be hoed by a specified date ... before the rains are expected. Another is that the banks of streams must be left uncultivated. There are also veterinary rules to prevent the spread of disease; in some districts these require cattle to be dipped once a week. Breaches of these rules lead to fines and in extreme cases to imprisonment. They are very unpopular. Their object is little understood because it lies in the long term and the African does not look very far ahead. It is indeed, the Government claim, because of the difficulty of making the African see for himself the advantages of soil conservation that it is necessary to enforce these rules by penalties and not simply to rely upon the education of the African up to higher agricultural standards.

39. The enforcement of these rules led to disputes and to a great deal of bitter feeling ... The Government contend that opposition to them was being deliberately fomented by [Nyasaland National] Congress leaders, who knew or ought to have known how necessary they are, simply in order to stir up anti-government feeling. Not all the rules are universally considered to be beneficial, even by well-informed opinion; and we have quite independent evidence that the Government was sometimes too rigid about their enforcement. Dr. Banda [leader of the Nyasaland National Congress] in his speeches did not disapprove of agricultural legislation as such but he strongly disapproved of its enforcement by punishment and not by persuasion. We have no doubt that in many districts Congress leaders made as much capital as they could out of any government action which was unpopular; and in this respect the agricultural rules were a very happy hunting ground.

Report of the Nyasaland Commission of Inquiry (Devlin Report), Cmd. 814, HMSO, 1959, p. 19.

(b)

		S. Rhodesia	N. Rhodesia	Nyasaland
European population:	1938	61,000	13,000	1,900
	1946	83,000	22,000	2,000
	1950	129,000	36,000	4,000
African population:	1950	1,960,000	1,849,000	2,330,000

The European and African populations of Southern Rhodesia, Northern Rhodesia and Nyasaland, 1938–50, [10], p. 83.

DOCUMENT 21   NATIONALISM AND THE PACE OF CONSTITUTIONAL DEVELOPMENT

This statement by a British official committee might suggest that Britain was no longer capable of dictating the pace of colonial political development by the 1950s.

... [C]onstitutional development is proceeding steadily in many parts of the Colonial Empire. This process cannot now be halted or reversed, and it is only to a limited extent that its pace can be controlled by the United Kingdom Government. Sometimes it may be possible to secure acceptance of a reasonable and beneficial delay in order to ensure a more orderly transition. But, in the main, the pace of constitutional change will be determined by the strength of nationalist feeling in the territory concerned. Political leaders who have obtained assurances of independence for their people normally expect that the promised independence will be attained within their own political lifetime; and, if they cannot satisfy their followers that satisfactory progress is being maintained towards that goal, their influence may be usurped by less responsible elements. No Party in this country can afford to have it said that, though it promised independence, it never meant to concede it. Any attempt to retard by artificial delays the progress of Colonial peoples towards independence would produce disastrous results. Among other consequences it would ensure that, when power had eventually been transferred, it would be handed over to a local leadership predisposed towards an anti-British policy.

Report by the Official Committee on Commonwealth Membership, 21 January 1954 [187, 2], p. 284 cited in [101].

DOCUMENT 22   COMPETING NATIONALISMS IN WEST AFRICA

As this political appreciation by the Governor of the Gold Coast illustrates, Kwame Nkrumah's Convention Peoples' Party (CPP) was far from representative of all the peoples of the Gold Coast.

6. The main event in the Gold Coast during the last few months has been the rise of the National Liberation Movement in Ashanti. This movement is aimed primarily against the C.P.P. Government. It was inspired partly by the fixing of the prices of cocoa at the same price as last year, ... but is directed against the over-centralisation of the Government in Accra and its control by the party bosses. The movement took as its platform 'Federation'; although its leaders have not yet admitted it, I think they are unaware what federation means, and they may well be satisfied with some form of devolution of power on a regional basis. Dr. Nkrumah is prepared to accept the establishment of regional councils as deliberative and consultative bodies. Invitations were issued by Dr. Nkrumah, early this month, to the N.L.M. and to the Asanteman Council [the Council of Chiefs in Ashanti] to discuss 'federation' and other differences of opinion between the N.L.M. and the Government. I have now heard that these invitations are being declined. The next step promises great interest and may prove to have a bearing on the date when the Gold Coast will earn its independence.

7. In the Northern Territories no overt support has appeared for the N.L.M., but a working agreement between Ashanti and the Northern Territories is not improbable as both of them have the same fears concerning centralised government in Accra.

Arden-Clarke to Lennox-Boyd, 22 December 1954, [188, 2], p. 107.

DOCUMENT 23   THE REVIVAL OF AMERICAN ANTI-COLONIALISM IN THE 1950S

American anti-colonialism, although somewhat dampened down in the early years of the Cold War, witnessed a revival in the mid-1950s under President Eisenhower's Secretary of State, John Foster Dulles.

2. ... [T]here has been a recrudescence of reports about anti-colonialism in a number of metropolitan newspapers (set off usually by the visible failure of French colonialism in Indo-China). ... Of the papers concerned the New York Times and the Washington Post have led the field in stressing the view that colonialism is obsolete, that Asian and African nationalism is the force with which the United States should associate itself, and that the United States can expose Soviet imperialism more effectively if it opposes colonialism of any

kind. And they have gone further than most in implying or even alleging that 'the State Department' holds similar views. ... Indeed there is substantial evidence that Dulles ... has become more inclined to see 'colonialism' as an obstacle to uniting the 'free' world against Communist aggression. In this he has been encouraged by certain groups in the State Department (especially the Policy Planning Staff) and at the Pentagon; who have been impressed by the unwillingness of the Indo-Chinese to fight for 'freedom' if this meant continued French domination.

J. H. A. Watson, British Embassy, Washington to M. C. G. Man, Foreign Office, 31 August 1954 [182, 1], p. 284.

DOCUMENT 24   **ANTI-COLONIALISM IN THE UNITED NATIONS: THE ROLE OF INDIA**

Anti-colonial attitudes became increasingly prevalent at the United Nations General Assembly as newly independent countries joined the organisation. India became an effective leader of this anti-colonial grouping.

5. ... India is much the most influential and persistent of the anti-colonial leaders in the United Nations and, we believe, the brains of the Arab/Asian bloc when it comes to evolving ways of embarrassing the Colonial powers. She has had so much intimate experience of our susceptibilities on Colonial issues that she is able to put a finger on our weak spots with unerring accuracy. It is safe to say that if India can be dissuaded from initiating or supporting a particular anti-Colonial manoeuvre, her friends in the Arab/Asian bloc are either so clumsy or so lacking in genuine concern with Colonial issues that we should have no difficulty in killing that manoeuvre in the lobby.

Sir J. Martin, Colonial Office to N. Pritchard, Commonwealth Relations Office, 7 August 1953 [182, 1], p. 333.

DOCUMENT 25   **ANGLO-AMERICAN COOPERATION IN AFRICA**

Following the talks of November 1958 between American Secretary of State, John Foster Dulles, and British Foreign Secretary, John Selwyn Lloyd, a document was drawn up by British officials which outlined the best means of the Western Alliance preventing Soviet penetration of Africa.

102. ... The pace of the advance towards independence has become rapid in much of Africa. France has granted all her colonies internal self-government, with the right, at least in theory, to opt for independence at any time; and the

Belgian Congo is likely to reach the same position in a short period. We ourselves have moved even faster in West Africa. But in the east and south the position is different. If, on the one hand, we retreat there too rapidly before the rising tide of Pan-Africanism, we shall run the risk of transferring power to local Governments before they are competent to exercise authority or to maintain stable and viable administration. We shall expose volatile and unsophisticated peoples to the insidious dangers of Communist penetration. And we shall jeopardise European interests and investments, which have made the major contribution to the development of large parts of Africa and can claim the main credit for the gradual improvement in the African standard of living. ... If, on the other hand, we are too intransigent in opposing African aspirations or, where European minorities are dominant, are too ready to appease them, we run the risk of being identified with the extreme racial doctrines of the Union of South Africa, of exacerbating African hostility towards the European and of provoking the African States, when they finally achieve independence – as in the end they must – to turn more readily towards the Soviet Union. ... The West therefore must seek to steer a middle course between these extremes, bearing well in mind that, while the Soviet Union will be alert to seize every opportunity to exploit our dilemma, Pan-Africanism in itself is not necessarily a force which we need regard with fear and suspicion. On the contrary, if we can avoid alienating it and can guide it on lines generally sympathetic to the free world, it may well prove in the longer term a strong, indigenous barrier to the penetration of Africa by the Soviet Union ...

... If Africa is to remain loyal to the Western cause, its economic interests must coincide with, and reinforce, its political sympathies; and one of the major problems of the relationship between the West and Africa will be to ensure an adequate flow of economic assistance, and particularly capital, through various channels to the newly emerging States. On any reckoning the amounts required will be considerable; and, if the Western Powers are unreasonably insensitive to the economic aspirations of independent Africa, the Governments of the new states may be compelled to turn to the Soviet Union for the assistance which they will certainly need. ...

'Africa: the Next Ten Years', December 1959, FO 371/137972 cited in [130].

DOCUMENT 26   THE COLD WAR AND THE 'WIND OF CHANGE'

After 1959, Harold Macmillan's government accelerated the pace of decolonisation – particularly in east and central Africa. Macmillan's famous 'wind of change' speech to the South African parliament in 1960 is notable for the stress placed on Cold War factors as justification for the new course.

The wind of change is blowing through this continent and, whether we like it or not, this growth of national consciousness is a political fact. We must all accept it as a fact, and our national policies must take account of it. ...

... As I see it the great issue in this second half of the twentieth century is whether the uncommitted peoples of Asia and Africa will swing to the East or to the West. Will they be drawn into the Communist camp? Or will the great experiments of self-government that are now being made in Asia and Africa, especially within the Commonwealth, prove so successful, and by their example so compelling, that the balance will come down in favour of freedom and order and justice?

Speech by Harold Macmillan to both Houses of the Parliament of the Union of South Africa, Cape Town, 3 February 1960, [187, 2], p. 525.

DOCUMENT 27   TENSIONS IN THE ANGLO-AMERICAN COALITION: THE EAST OF SUEZ DECISION

On 12 January 1968 Labour Foreign Secretary, George Brown, reported to the Cabinet on American reaction at the decision to withdraw British forces from 'east of Suez'. Brown's report was recorded by the Lord President of the Council, Richard Crossman, in his diary.

... George Brown had bustled into the room and we decided he should give us a special report on his interview with Dean Rusk [American Secretary of State] and on the message from L. B. J. [Lyndon B. Johnson, the President of the United States] which had arrived at the F. O. this morning. ... [H]e sat down and gave us in his most dramatic and most incoherent way a half-hour description of the appalling onslaught to which he had been submitted, first by Dean Rusk and then by a State Department official whose theme had been, 'Be British, George, be British – how can you betray us?' He told us that he had faithfully reported the decision to leave Singapore by 1970-71 ... They had expressed nothing but horror and consternation. ... The main American complaint was not about the withdrawal from the Far East but about the decision to leave the Persian Gulf. When the Americans had made this clear George Brown had explained that it didn't cost us much more to hold the Gulf if we were in Singapore and Malaya but that as we had to abandon Singapore and Malaya we couldn't hold the Gulf without incurring colossal expense. His contention was that irreparable damage had been done by his having to make this statement at all and having to tell the Americans of our decisions. ...

R. H. S. Crossman, *The Diaries of a Cabinet Minister*, vol. 2, Hamish Hamilton and Jonathan Cape, 1976, pp. 646–7 cited in [6].

DOCUMENT 28   PRESIDENT EISENHOWER AND THE SUEZ
CRISIS

*The Eisenhower administration in Washington was consistently against the
use of force to solve the Suez canal dispute of 1956.*

I really do not see how a successful result could be achieved by forcible
means. The use of force would, it seems to me, vastly increase the area of
jeopardy. I do not see how the economy of Western Europe can long survive
the burden of prolonged military operations, as well as the denial of Near
East oil. Also the peoples of the Near East and of North Africa and, to some
extent, of all of Asia and all of Africa, would be consolidated against the West
to a degree which, I fear, could not be overcome in a generation, and perhaps
not even in a century, particularly having in mind the capacity of the Russians
to make mischief ...

Eisenhower to Eden, 2 September 1956, [143], p. 119.

DOCUMENT 29   THE NECESSITY FOR AMERICAN AID AND
THE WITHDRAWAL FROM SUEZ

*The Suez invasion set off a disastrous run on the pound resulting in a net loss
of over $300 million of the gold and dollar reserves during November 1956.
On 28 November the Chancellor of the Exchequer, Harold Macmillan,
explained to the Cabinet that without American financial assistance, which
would, in turn, be conditional upon Britain and France's withdrawal from
Egypt, the British economy faced grave difficulties.*

The Chancellor of the Exchequer said that it would be necessary to announce
early in the following week the losses of gold and dollars which we had
sustained during November. This statement would reveal a very serious drain
on the reserves and would be a considerable shock both to public opinion in
this country and to international confidence in sterling. It was therefore
important that we should be able to announce at the same time that we were
taking action to reinforce the reserves both by recourse to the International
Monetary Fund and in other ways. For this purpose the goodwill of the
United States Government was necessary; and it was evident that this good
will could not be obtained without an immediate and unconditional undertaking to withdraw the Anglo-French force from Port Said. He therefore
favoured a prompt announcement of our intention to withdraw this force,
justifying this action on the ground that we had now achieved the purpose for
which we had originally launched the Anglo-French military operation
against Egypt and that we were content to leave the United Nations, backed
by the United States, the responsibility, which the General Assembly could

now be deemed to have accepted for settling the problems of the Middle East. ...

Minutes of Cabinet Meeting of 28 November 1956, [183], p. 142–3.

DOCUMENT 30   **THE LESSONS OF SUEZ**

Shortly before his resignation, Prime Minister Eden called for a general review of Britain's position in the light of American intervention during the Suez crisis.

We have to try to assess the lessons of Suez. The first is that if we are to play an independent part in the world, even on a more modest scale than we have done heretofore, we must ensure our financial and economic independence. Since we have no raw materials but coal, this means that we must excel in technical knowledge. This in its turn affects our military plans.

Too many of our scientists are working for the fighting Services. I think that I have seen a figure of two-thirds. Anything of this order cannot be accepted at the present time. On the other hand, some progress with the military aspects of the development of the hydrogen bomb can no doubt be useful for civil purposes also. It seems therefore that we have need to keep the balance between civil and military development, leaning rather towards the former in our nuclear programme.

In the strategic sphere we have to do some re-thinking about our areas of influence and the military bases on which they must rest. Some of the latter seem of doubtful value in the light of our Suez experience.

What return for instance do we get for our armoured division in Tripoli and Libya? If the purpose is to prevent this part of North Africa falling under Egyptian dominion, could that not be assured more cheaply? We shall still need the air facilities at El Adem as well as Cyprus if we are to be sure of reaching the Persian Gulf, which is today our most important overseas commitment. But do we need armour in Tripoli itself? And would not a smaller garrison be sufficient if one is needed at all? If we apply the same considerations to the Indian Ocean, can we not now dispense with the Ceylon Naval base altogether, using the Maldives instead for the air? Can we not increase the integration of the Services so far as concerns our requirements at Singapore? Do we need so many troops in Malaya? ...

One of the lessons of Suez is that we need a smaller force that is more mobile and more modern in its equipment. This probably means that we have in proportion to our total army too much armour and too much infantry and too small a paratroop force. We cannot contemplate keeping an army in Germany which is numerically much more that half its present numbers and the cost will have to come down proportionately. Mobility and quality in training rather than numbers would be our need.

[Passage deleted and retained under Section 3(4).]

... The most anxious fact on the home front is I think the alarming increase in the cost of the welfare state. Some of this, e.g. education, is a necessary part of our effort to maintain a leading position in new industrial developments. Other aspects of this spending are less directly related to our struggle for existence. I have long been anxious ... to do something to encourage our young and gifted leaders in science and industry to stay with us. The present burden of taxation leaves them with little incentive except patriotism. We shall not have adjusted our problems until the younger generation here can feel that they live in a community which is leading in industrial development and can reasonably expect a fair reward for their brains and application.

The conclusion of all this is surely that we must review our world position and our domestic capacity more searchingly in the light of the Suez experience, which has not so much changed our fortunes as revealed realities. While the consequences of this may be to determine us to work more closely with Europe, carrying with us, we hope our closest friends in the Commonwealth in such development, here too we must be under no illusion. Europe will not welcome us simply because at the moment it may appear to suit us to look to them. The timing and conviction of our approach may be decisive in their influence on those with whom we plan to work.

Public Record Office, PREM 11/1138, Note by Sir Anthony Eden, 28 September 1956.

DOCUMENT 31 DIFFERENCES IN ANGLO-FRENCH APPROACHES TO DECOLONISATION

A Colonial Office official explains the fundamental differences between French and British colonial policies.

9. Whereas we aim at developing political institutions in colonial territories and gradually handing over power to them, the French, while they administer West and Equatorial Africa through groups of territories each with its own Government and Assembly, seek to link these territories constitutionally to France itself through the Union Française. French colonial policy, moreover, has always had as one of its principal objectives to create good Frenchmen; hence the emphasis of the rights of the individual as a citizen of France as opposed to our emphasis on the political advancement of each colonial territory as a whole. The French have Assemblies in West Africa and in French Equatorial Africa and in each of the territories which compose them; these Assemblies have considerable powers in finance but only limited powers of legislation. Control over finance, administrative action and legislation is to a great degree concentrated in Paris. Each of the territories selects deputies to both Houses of the French Parliament and to the Assembly of the Union Française in Versailles.

10. We and the French thus have quite different policies in West Africa. We aim at establishing self-governing institutions in each colonial territory; the French aim at strengthening the organic link between the territories and France. Our policy in the constitutional sphere is to devolve; theirs is to centralise. Clearly the French and British policies cannot be harmonised unless one of them is modified and ... ours could not be modified without endangering our whole position in West Africa and departing from the well accepted method of political evolution of the British Commonwealth. ...

Memorandum by Andrew Cohen, 20 November 1951 [182, 1], pp. 299–300.

CHRONOLOGY OF INDEPENDENCE FOR BRITISH DEPENDENCIES

1946	Trans-Jordan (Jordan)
1947	India; Pakistan (East Pakistan seceded to become Bangladesh in 1971)
1948	Ceylon (Sri Lanka); Burma (Myanmar); Palestine (Israel)
1956	Sudan (formerly ruled as an Anglo-Egyptian condominium)
1957	Gold Coast (Ghana); Malaya
1960	British Somaliland (joined Somalia); Cyprus; Nigeria
1961	Sierra Leone; Cameroons (joined Nigeria and Cameroun); Tanganyika (Tanzania); Kuwait
1962	Western Samoa (formerly administered by New Zealand); Jamaica; Trinidad and Tobago; Uganda
1963	Zanzibar (joined Tanganyika to become Tanzania); Kenya; Sabah, Sarawak and Singapore as Malaysia (with Malaya)
1964	Nyasaland (Malawi); Malta; Northern Rhodesia (Zambia)
1965	Singapore (left Malaysia); Gambia; Maldives
1966	British Guiana (Guyana); Bechuanaland (Botswana); Basutoland (Lesotho); Barbados
1967	Aden (South Yemen)
1968	Mauritius; Swaziland; Nauru (formerly administered by Australia, Britain and New Zealand).
1970	Tonga; Fiji
1971	Bahrain; Qatar; United Arab Emirates
1973	The Bahamas
1974	Grenada
1975	British New Guinea (Papua New Guinea; formerly administered by Australia)
1976	Seychelles
1978	Dominica; Solomon Islands; Ellice Islands (Tuvalu)
1979	St Vincent and the Grenadines; St. Lucia; Gilbert Islands (Kiribati)
1980	Southern Rhodesia (Zimbabwe); New Hebrides (Vanuatu; formerly ruled as an Anglo-French condominium)
1981	Belize; Antigua and Barbuda
1983	St Christopher and Nevis (St Kitts and Nevis)
1984	Brunei
1997	Hong Kong (returned to China)

Adapted from [6 p. vii; 17 pp. 342–3].

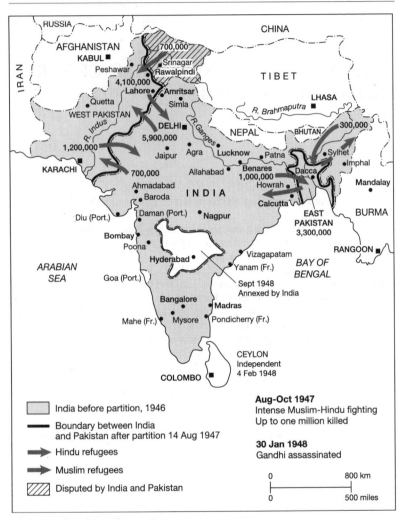

Map 1. Indian partition, 1947
Source: R. F. Holland, *European Decolonization: An Introductory Survey 1918–1981*, Macmillan, 1985, p. 80

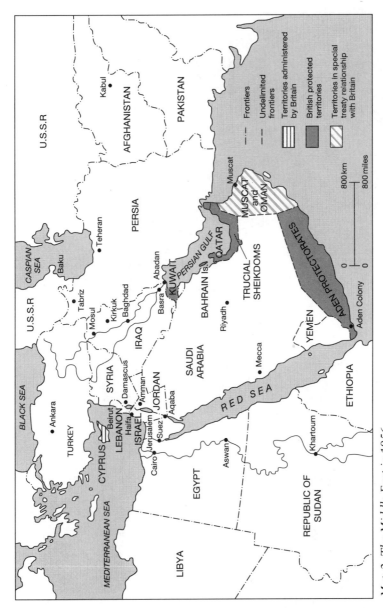

Map 2. The Middle East in 1956
Source: R. F. Holland, *European Decolonization: An Introductory Survey 1918–1981*, Macmillan, 1985, p. 194

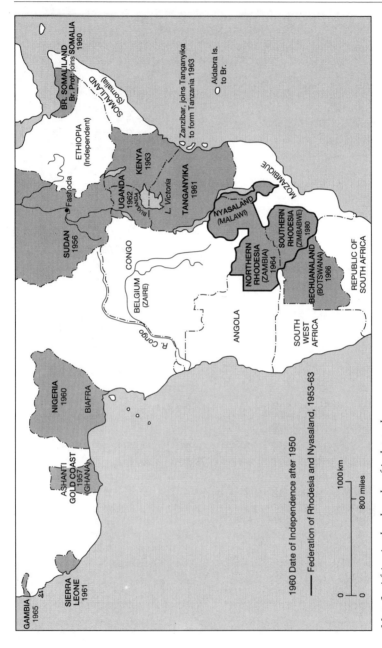

Map 3. Africa in the decade of independence
Source: T. O. Lloyd, *The British Empire, 1558–1983*, Oxford University Press, 1984, p. 350.

GUIDE TO MAIN CHARACTERS

Abdul Rahman, Tunku (1903–90): Malayan nationalist and politician; President United Malays National Organisation, 1951; leader of Alliance of Malayan communal parties, 1952; Chief Minister, Federation of Malaya, 1955; Prime Minister, Malaya/Malaysia, 1957–70.

Attlee, Clement (1883–1967): British Labour politician; Dominions Secretary (1942–3) and Deputy Prime Minister (1942–5) in Churchill's coalition; Prime Minister, 1945–51; Leader of Opposition, 1951–5.

Azikiwe, Nnamdi (1904–): Nigerian politician; Secretary (1944–6) and President (1946–60) of the National Council of Nigeria and the Cameroons; Governor-General of Nigeria, 1960; President of Nigeria, 1963–6.

Bevin, Ernest (1881–1951): British Labour politician and trade unionist; became a Labour MP in 1940; Minister of Labour and National Service (1940–5) in Churchill's coalition; Foreign Secretary, 1945–51.

Blundell, Michael (1907–1993): White Kenyan farmer, businessman and politician; Member for Agriculture in Kenyan Legislative Council, 1955–9, 1961–3; leader of New Kenya Group, 1959–63.

Churchill, Sir Winston (1874–1965): British Conservative politician and statesman; Prime Minister and Minister of Defence, 1940–5; Leader of Opposition, 1945–51; Prime Minister, 1951–5.

Cohen, Andrew (1909–1968): British administrator; Assistant Secretary, Colonial Office, 1943–7; Assistant Under-Secretary of State and Head of Africa Division, Colonial Office, 1947–1952; Governor of Uganda, 1952–7.

Cripps, Sir Stafford (1889–1952): British Labour politician; cabinet minister in the Churchill coalition during the Second World War; President of the Board of Trade, 1945–7; led Cabinet mission to India, 1946; Minister for Economic Affairs, 1947; Chancellor of the Exchequer, 1947–50.

Dulles, John Foster (1888–1959): US politician; US delegate to the General Assembly of the United Nations, 1945–53; US Secretary of State in Eisenhower's administration, 1953–9.

Eden, Sir Anthony (1897–1977): British Conservative politician; Foreign Secretary, 1935–8 (resigned over Chamberlain government's recognition of Italy's conquest of Ethiopia); Dominions Secretary, 1939–40; Secretary for War, 1940; Foreign Secretary, 1940–5, 1951–5; Prime Minister, 1955–7.

Eisenhower, Dwight David (1890–1969): US general and politician; Supreme Commander NATO forces in Europe, 1950–2; President of the US, 1953–61.

Gandhi, Mohandas Karamachand ('Mahatma') (1869–1948): Indian nationalist; leader of the Indian National Congress after returning to India from South Africa in 1914; led major campaigns of non-violent, non-cooperation (or civil disobedience) against British rule in India during the interwar years; negotiated with 1946 Cabinet mission on Indian constitution; assassinated in 1948 by a Hindu extremist following his attempts to end Hindu-Muslim violence in Bengal.

Gaulle, Charles de (1898–1970): French general and politician; leader of the Free French during the Second World War; head of French Provisional Government, 1944–6; last Prime Minister of French Fourth Republic, 1958; first President Fifth Republic, 1959–69.

Jinnah, Mohammed Ali (1876–1948): Indian Muslim politician; leader of Muslim League and Pakistan separatist movement after 1935; Governor-General of Pakistan, 1947.

Jones, Arthur Creech (1891–1964): British Labour politician; chairman of Fabian Colonial Bureau during the Second World War; Colonial Secretary, 1946–50.

Lennox-Boyd, Alan (1904–83): British Conservative politician; Colonial Secretary, 1954–9.

Kennedy, John Fitzgerald (1917–63): President of US, 1960–3.

Kenyatta, Jomo (1891–1978): Kenyan nationalist and politician; President of the Kenya African Union, 1946; detained 1952–61 for alleged involvement in Mau Mau uprising; elected President of the Kenya African National Union, 1960; Prime Minister of independent Kenya, 1963; President of the Republic of Kenya, 1964–78.

Khrushchev, Nikita (1894–1971): Soviet politician; General-Secretary of the Communist Party of the Soviet Union, 1953–64.

MacDonald, Malcolm (1901–81): British Labour politician and administrator; Colonial Secretary, 1935, 1938–40; Commissioner-General in Southeast Asia, 1948–55; High Commissioner, India, 1955–60; Governor, 1963, Governor-General, 1963–4, and High Commissioner, 1964–5, Kenya.

Macleod, Iain (1913–70): British Conservative politician; Minister of Health, 1952–5; Minister of Labour and National Service, 1955–9; Colonial Secretary, 1959–61.

Macmillan, Harold (1892–1986): British Conservative politician; cabinet minister in Churchill coalition during Second World War; Conservative Minister of Housing and Local Government, 1951–4; Minister of Defence, 1954–5; Foreign Secretary, 1955; Chancellor of the Exchequer, 1955–7; Prime Minister, 1957–63.

Nasser, Gamal Abdel (1918–70): Egyptian politician and army officer; involved in the military coup of 1952 which overthrew King Farouk; Prime Minister of Egypt, 1954–6; President, 1956–70.

Nehru, Jawaharlal ('Pandit') (1889–1964): Indian nationalist and politician; joined Indian Congress Committee in 1918 and became a disciple of Gandhi; elected President of the Indian National Congress, 1929; negotiated Indian independence with the British, 1946–7; Prime Minister of India, 1947–64.

Nkrumah, Kwame (1909–72): Ghanaian nationalist and politician; Secretary-General of the United Gold Coast Convention, 1947; formed Convention People's Party, 1949; Leader of Government Business, Gold Coast, 1951; Prime Minister of the Gold Coast (Ghana), 1952–60; President of the Republic of Ghana, 1960–6.

Roosevelt, Franklin Delano (1882–1945): President of the US, 1933–45.

Stalin, Joseph (1879–1953): Soviet dictator; General-Secretary of the Central Committee of the Communist Party of the Soviet Union, 1922–53; also occupied other key positions in the Soviet Union which allowed for the accumulation of remarkable personal power (particularly after the death of Lenin in 1924).

Wilson, Harold (1916–1995): British Labour politician; President of the Board of Trade, 1947–51; leader of the Labour Party, 1963; Prime Minister, 1964–70, 1974–76.

BIBLIOGRAPHY

GENERAL SURVEYS

1   Birmingham, D., *The Decolonization of Africa*, UCL Press, 1995.
2   Cain, P. J. and Hopkins, A. G., *British Imperialism: Crisis and Deconstruction, 1914–1990*, Longman, 1993.
3   Darwin, J., 'Imperialism in Decline?', *Historical Journal*, xxiii, 1980.
4   Darwin, J., 'British Decolonization since 1945: A Pattern or a Puzzle?', *Journal of Imperial and Commonwealth History*, xii, 1984.
5   Darwin, J., *Britain and Decolonisation*, Macmillan, 1988.
6   Darwin, J., *The End of the British Empire: The Historical Debate*, Blackwell, 1991.
7   Havinden, M. and Meredith, D., *Colonialism and Development: Britain and Its Tropical Colonies, 1850–1960*, Routledge, 1993.
8   Gallagher, J., *The Decline, Revival and Fall of the British Empire*, Cambridge University Press, 1982.
9   Goldsworthy, D., *Colonial Issues in British Politics, 1945–1961*, Oxford University Press, 1971.
10 Hargreaves, J. D., *Decolonization in Africa*, Longman, 1st edn., 1988; 2nd edn, 1996.
11 Holland, R. F., 'The Imperial Factor in British Strategies from Attlee to Macmillan, 1945–63', *Journal of Imperial and Commonwealth History*, xii, 1984.
12 Holland, R. F., *European Decolonization, 1918–1981: An Introductory Survey*, Macmillan, 1985.
13 Holland, R. F., *The Pursuit of Greatness: Britain and the World Role, 1900– 1970*, Fontana, 1991.
14 Kahler, M., *Decolonization in Britain and France*, Princeton University Press, 1984.
15 Morgan, D. J., *The Official History of Colonial Development*, 5 Volumes, Macmillan, 1980.
16 Ovendale, R., *Britain, the United States and the Transfer of Power in the Middle East, 1945–1962*, Leicester University Press, 1996.
17 Porter, B., *The Lion's Share: A Short History of British Imperialism, 1850– 1995*, 3rd edn, Longman, 1996.

18   Tomlinson, B. R., 'The Contraction of England: National Decline and Loss of Empire', *Journal of Imperial and Commonwealth History*, xi, 1982.

19   Wilson, H. S., *African Decolonization*, Edward Arnold, 1994.

THE LABOUR GOVERNMENTS AND THE EMPIRE, 1945–51

20   Barnett, C., *The Lost Victory*, Macmillan, 1995.

21   Butler, L. J., 'The Ambiguities of British Colonial Development Policy, 1938– 48', in Gorst, A., Johnman, L. and Lucas, W. S. eds, *Contemporary British History, 1931–61: Politics and the Limits of Policy*, Pinter, 1991.

22   Butler, L. J., *Industrialisation and the British Colonial State: West Africa, 1939–1951*, Frank Cass, 1997.

23   Cohen, M. J., *Palestine and the Great Powers, 1945–1948*, Princeton University Press, 1982.

24   Cohen, M. J., *Fighting World War Three from the Middle East: Allied Contingency Plans, 1945–1954*, Frank Cass, 1997.

25   Darby, P., *British Defence Policy East of Suez, 1947–68*, Oxford University Press, 1973.

26   Fieldhouse, D. K., 'The Labour Governments and the Empire-Commonwealth, 1945–51' in Ovendale, R. ed., *The Foreign Policies of the British Labour Governments, 1945–1951*, Leicester University Press, 1984.

27   Hinds, A. E., 'Sterling and Imperial Policy, 1945–51', *Journal of Imperial and Commonwealth History*, xv, 1987.

28   Hinds, A. E., 'Imperial Policy and Colonial Sterling Balances, 1943– 56', *Journal of Imperial and Commonwealth History*, xix, 1991.

29   Hyam, R., 'The Geopolitical Origins of the Central African Federation: Britain, Rhodesia and South Africa, 1948–1953', *Historical Journal*, xxx, 1987.

30   Hyam, R., 'Africa and the Labour Government, 1945–51', *Journal of Imperial and Commonwealth History*, xvi, 1988.

31   Hyam, R., 'Introduction' in Hyam, R. ed., *The Labour Government and the End of Empire, 1945–1951*, Volume One, HMSO, 1992.

32   Kent, J., 'The British Empire and the Origins of the Cold War, 1944– 49' in Deighton, A. ed., *Britain and the First Cold War*, Macmillan, 1990.

33   Kent, J., *British Imperial Strategy and the Origins of the Cold War, 1944–49*, Leicester University Press, 1993.

34   Kingston, P., *Britain and the Politics of Modernization in the Middle East*, Cambridge University Press, 1996.

35   Krozewski, G., 'Sterling, the "Minor" Territories, and the End of Formal Empire, 1939–58', *Economic History Review*, xlvi, 1993.

36   Louis, W. R., *The British Empire in the Middle East, 1945–1951*, Clarendon, 1984.

37   Low, D. A. and Lonsdale, J. M., 'Introduction: Towards the New Order' in Low, D. A. and Smith, A. eds, *History of East Africa*, Volume 3, Clarendon Press, 1976.

38   Moore, R. J., *Escape from Empire: The Attlee Government and the Indian Problem*, Clarendon Press, 1983.

39   Moore, R. J., *Making the New Commonwealth*, Clarendon Press, 1987.

40   Morgan, K. O., *Labour in Power, 1945–1951*, Oxford University Press, 1985.

41   Murfett, M. H., *In Jeopardy: The Royal Navy and British Far Eastern Defence Policy, 1945–1951*, Oxford University Press, 1995.

42   Newton, S., 'Britain, the Sterling Area and European Integration, 1945–50', *Journal of Imperial and Commonwealth History*, xiii, 1985.

43   Ovendale, R., *Britain, the United States, and the End of the Palestine Mandate, 1942–1948*, Royal Historical Society, 1989.

44   Owen, N., '"Responsibility without Power": the Attlee Governments and the End of British Rule in India', in Tiratsoo, N. ed., *The Attlee Years*, Pinter, 1991.

45   Pearce, R. D., *The Turning Point in Africa: British Colonial Policy, 1938– 1948*, Frank Cass, 1982.

46   Remme, T., *Britain and Regional Cooperation in Southeast Asia, 1945–49*, Routledge, 1995.

47   Robinson, R. E., 'Andrew Cohen and the Transfer of Power in Tropical Africa, 1940–51' in Morris-Jones, W. H. and Fischer, G. eds, *Decolonisation and After*, Frank Cass, 1980.

48   Smith, S. C., *British Relations with the Malay Rulers from Decentralization to Malayan Independence, 1930–1957*, Oxford University Press, 1995.

49   Stockwell, A. J., 'British Imperial Policy and Decolonization in Malaya, 1942– 52', *Journal of Imperial and Commonwealth History*, xiii, 1984.

50   Stockwell, A. J., 'Introduction' in Stockwell, A. J. ed., *Malaya*, HMSO, Volume One, 1995.

51   Tang, J. T. H., 'From Empire Defence to Imperial Retreat: Britain's Postwar China Policy and the Decolonization of Hong Kong', *Modern Asian Studies*, xxviii, 1994.

52   Tomlinson, B. R., *The Political Economy of the Raj, 1914–47: The Economics of Decolonization in India*, Macmillan, 1979.

53   Tsang, S. Y., *Democracy Shelved: Great Britain, China, and Attempts at Constitutional Reform in Hong Kong, 1945–1952*, Oxford University Press, 1988.

54   Westcott, N. J., 'Closer Union and the Future of East Africa, 1939–1948', *Journal of Imperial and Commonwealth History*, x, 1981.

IMPERIAL POLICY IN THE 1950s AND 1960s

55   Butler, L. J., 'Winds of Change: Britain, Europe and the Common-wealth, 1959–61' in Brivati, B. and Jones, H. eds, *From Reconstruction to Integration: Britain and Europe since 1945*, Leicester University Press, 1993.

56   Carruthers, S. L., *Winning Hearts and Minds: British Governments, the Media and Colonial Counterinsurgency, 1944–1960*, Leicester University Press, 1995.

57   Peter Catterall ed., 'The East of Suez Decision', *Contemporary Record*, vii, 1993.

58   Darwin, J., 'The Fear of Falling: British Politics and Imperial Decline Since 1900', *Transactions of the Royal Historical Society*, xxxvi, 1986.

59   Feinstein, C. H., 'The end of empire and the golden age' in Clarke, P. and Trebilcock, C. eds, *Understanding Decline: Perceptions and Realities of British Economic Performance*, Cambridge University Press, 1997.

60   Fieldhouse, D. K., *Unilever Overseas: The Anatomy of a Multinational, 1895– 1965*, Croom Helm, 1978.

61   Fieldhouse, D. K., *Black Africa, 1945–1980: Economic Decolonization and Arrested Development*, Unwin Hyman, 1986.

62   Goldsworthy, D., 'Keeping Change Within Bounds: Aspects of Colonial Policy During the Churchill and Eden Governments, 1951–57', *Journal of Imperial and Commonwealth History*, xviii, 1990.

63   Goldsworthy, D., 'Introduction' in Goldsworthy, D. ed., *The Conservative Government and the End of Empire, 1951–1957*, Volume One, HMSO, 1994.

64   Gow, M., 'Britain, America and the Bomb' in Dilks, D. ed., *Retreat from Power: Studies in Britain's Foreign Policy of the Twentieth Century: Volume Two After 1939*, Macmillan, 1981.

65   Hopkins, T., 'Macmillan's Audit of Empire, 1957' in Clarke, P. and Trebilcock, C. eds, *Understanding Decline: Perceptions and Realities of British Economic Performance*, Cambridge University Press, 1997.

66   Howe, S., *Anticolonialism in British Politics: the Left and the End of Empire, 1918–1964*, Clarendon Press, 1993.

67   Kyriakides, K. A., 'The Decolonization Treaties of 1960 and the Preservation of British Strategic Interests in Post-Colonial Cyprus', unpublished seminar paper, Institute of Commonwealth Studies, University of London, 1994.

68   Lau Siu-Kai, 'Decolonisation à la Hong Kong: Britain's Search for Governability and Exit with Glory', *Journal of Commonwealth and Comparative Politics*, xxxv, 1997.

69   McIntyre, W. D., 'The Admission of Small States to the Commonwealth', *Journal of Imperial and Commonwealth History*, xxiv, 1996.

70   MacKenzie, J. M., *Propaganda and Empire: the Manipulation of British Public Opinion, 1880–1960*, Manchester University Press, 1984.
71   Magdoff, H., 'Imperialism without Colonies' in Owen, R. and Sutcliffe, B. eds, *Studies in the Theory of Imperialism*, Longman, 1972.
72   Marshall, P. J., 'Imperial Britain', *Journal of Imperial and Commonwealth History*, xxiii, 1995.
73   Murphy, P., *Party Politics and Decolonization: The Conservative Party and British Colonial Policy in Tropical Africa, 1951–1964*, Clarendon Press, 1995.
74   Ovendale, R., 'Macmillan and the Wind of Change in Africa, 1957–1960', *Historical Journal*, xxxviii, 1995.
75   Schenk, C. R., *Britain and the Sterling Area: From Devaluation to Convertibility in the 1950s*, Routledge, 1994.
76   Schenk, C. R., 'Decolonization and European Economic Integration: The Free Trade Area Negotiations, 1956–8', *Journal of Imperial and Commonwealth History*, xxiv, 1996.
77   Stockwell, S., 'British Business, Politics and Decolonisation in the Gold Coast, c. 1945–60', D. Phil. thesis, Oxford University, 1993.
78   Tignor, R. L., *Capitalism and Nationalism at the End of Empire: State and Business in Decolonizing Egypt, Nigeria, and Kenya, 1945–1963*, Princeton University Press, 1998.
79   Wasserman, G., *Politics of Decolonization: Kenya Europeans and the Land Issue, 1960–1965*, Cambridge University Press, 1976.
80   White, N. J., *Business, Government, and the End of Empire: Malaya, 1942–1957*, Oxford University Press, 1996.
81   Wrigley, C., 'Now you see it, now you don't: Harold Wilson and Labour's Foreign Policy, 1964–70' in Coopey, R., Fielding, S. and Tiratsoo, N. eds, *The Wilson Governments, 1964–1970*, Pinter, 1993.
82   Young, J. W., 'Britain and the EEC, 1956–73: an Overview' in Brivati, B. and Jones, H. eds, *From Reconstruction to Integration: Britain and Europe since 1945*, Leicester University Press, 1993.

COLONIAL NATIONALISM

83   Anderson, B., *Imagined Communities*, Verso, 1983.
84   Birmingham, D. and Ranger, T., 'Settlers and Liberators in the South' in Birmingham, D. and Martin, P., *History of Central Africa: Volume Two*, Longman, 1983.
85   Boahen, A. A., *African Perspectives on Colonialism*, James Currey, 1989.
86   Brown, J., *Modern India*, Oxford University Press, 1985.
87   Christie, C., *A Modern History of Southeast Asia: Decolonization, Nationalism and Separatism*, I. B. Tauris, 1996.
88   Darwin, J., 'The Central African Emergency, 1959', *Journal of Imperial and Commonwealth History*, xxi, 1993.

89 Füredi, F., *Colonial Wars and the Politics of Third World Nationalism*, I. B. Tauris, 1994.
90 Gallagher, J. and Robinson, R., 'The Imperialism of Free Trade', *Economic History Review*, vi, 1953.
91 Gallagher, J. and Seal, A., 'Britain and India between the Wars', *Modern Asian Studies*, xv, 1981.
92 Geiger, S., 'Women and African Nationalism', *Journal of Women's History*, ii, 1990.
93 Hargreaves, J. D., *The End of Colonial Rule in West Africa*, Macmillan, 1979.
94 Harper, T. N., 'The Colonial Inheritance: State and Society in Malaya, 1945–1957', Ph. D. thesis, Cambridge University, 1991.
95 Holland, R. F., 'Never, Never Land: British Colonial Policy and the Roots of Violence in Cyprus, 1950–54', *Journal of Imperial and Commonwealth History*, xxi, 1993.
96 Hopkins, A. G., *An Economic History of West Africa*, Longman, 1973.
97 Howe, S., 'When the Sun Did Set', *Times Higher Educational Supplement*, November 13, 1992.
98 Iliffe, J., *A Modern History of Tanganyika*, Cambridge University Press, 1979.
99 Killingray, D., 'Soldiers, Ex-Servicemen, and Politics in the Gold Coast, 1939–50', *The Journal of Modern African Studies*, xxi, 1983.
100 Lonsdale, J., 'Some Origins of Nationalism in East Africa', *Journal of African History*, ix, 1968.
101 Low, D. A., *Eclipse of Empire*, Cambridge University Press, 1991.
102 Milner, A., *The Invention of Politics in Colonial Malaya*, Cambridge University Press, 1994.
103 Ranger, T. O., 'African Reactions to the Imposition of Colonial Rule in East and Central Africa' in Gann, L. and Duignan, P. eds, *Colonialism in Africa, 1870–1960: Volume One*, Cambridge University Press, 1969.
104 Ranger, T. O., *Peasant Consciousness and Guerrilla War in Zimbabwe*, 1985.
105 Rathbone, R., 'The Transfer of Power in Ghana, 1945–1957', Ph.D. thesis, London University, 1968.
106 Rathbone, R., 'Introduction' in Rathbone, R. ed., *Ghana*, Volume One, HMSO, 1992.
107 Robinson, R., 'Non-European Foundations of European Imperialism: Sketch for a Theory of Collaboration' in Owen, R. and Sutcliffe, B. eds, *Studies in the Theory of Imperialism*, Longman, 1972.
108 Rizvi, G., 'Transfer of Power in India: A "Re-statement" of an Alternative Approach', *Journal of Imperial and Commonwealth History*, xii, 1984.
109 Sarkar, S., *Modern India, 1885–1947*, Macmillan, 1989.
110 Seal, A., 'Imperialism and nationalism in India', *Modern Asian Studies*, vii, 1973.

111   Stockwell, A. J. 'South-East Asia in War and Peace: the End of European Colonial Empires' in Tarling, N. ed., *The Cambridge History of South-East Asia. Vol. II.* Cambridge University Press, 1992.

112   Stubbs, R., *Hearts and Minds in Guerrilla Warfare: The Malayan Emergency, 1948–1960,* Oxford University Press, 1989.

113   Throup, D., *Economic and Social Origins of Mau Mau, 1945–53,* James Currey, 1988.

114   Throup, D., 'The Historiography of Decolonization', unpublished seminar paper, Institute of Commonwealth Studies, University of London, 31 January 1991.

115   Young, M. C., 'Nationalism, Ethnicity and Class in Africa: A Retrospective', *Cahiers d'Études Africaines,* ciii, 1986.

INTERNATIONAL FACTORS

116   Balfour-Paul, G., *The End of Empire in the Middle East,* Cambridge University Press, 1991.

117   Beloff, M., 'The Consequences on US-British relations of the dissolution of the British empire and the assumption of world-wide commitments by the United States — a British view' in Bull, H. and Louis, W. R. eds, *The 'Special Relationship': Anglo-American Relations Since 1945,* Clarendon Press, 1986.

118   Bill, J. A. and Louis, W. R. eds, *Mussadiq, Iranian Nationalism and Oil,* Austin, Texas, 1988.

119   Darby, P., *Three Faces of Imperialism: British and American Approaches to Asia and Africa, 1870–1970,* Yale University Press, 1987.

120   Darwin, J., 'Decolonisation and World Politics' in Lowe, D. ed., *Australia and the End of Empires,* Deakin University Press, 1996.

121   Duignan, P. and Gann, L. H., *The United States and Africa: A History,* Cambridge University Press, 1984.

122   Dunbabin, J. P. D., *International Relations since 1945. Volume 2: The Post-Imperial Age,* Longman, 1994

123   James, A., *Britain and the Congo Crisis, 1960–1963,* Macmillan, 1996.

124   Kahler, M., 'The United States and the Third World' in Brown, L. C. ed., *Centerstage: American Diplomacy since World War II,* Holmes & Meier, 1990.

125   Kennedy, P., *The Rise and Fall of the Great Powers,* Unwin Hyman, 1988.

126   Kolko, G., *The Politics of War,* Vintage Books, 1986.

127   Louis, W. R., *Imperialism At Bay, 1941–1945: The United States and the Decolonization of the British Empire,* Clarendon Press, 1977.

128   Louis, W. R., 'American Anti-Colonialism and the Dissolution of the British Empire', *International Afffairs,* lxi, 1985.

129   Louis, W. R. and Robinson, R., 'The United States and the Liquidation of the British Empire in Tropical Africa, 1941–1951' in Gifford, P.

and Louis, W. R. eds, *The Transfer of Power in Africa: Decoloniza-tion, 1940–1960*, Yale University Press, 1982.
130 Louis, W. R. and Robinson, R., 'The Imperialism of Decolonization', *Journal of Imperial and Commonwealth History*, xxii, 1994.
131 Louis, W. R. and Stookey, R. W. eds, *The End of the Palestine Man-date*, Austin, Texas, 1986.
132 Löwenthal, R., 'The Soviet Union and the Third World: From Anti-Imperialism to Counter-Imperialism' in Bull, H. and Watson, A. eds, *The Expansion of International Society*, Clarendon Press, 1984.
133 Mahoney, R. D., *J. F. K. Ordeal in Africa*, Oxford University Press, 1984.
134 Porritt, V., *British Colonial Rule in Sarawak, 1946–1963*, Oxford University Press, 1997.
135 Rotter, A., *The Path to Vietnam: Origins of the American Commitment to Southeast Asia*, Cornell University Press, 1987.
136 Thorne, C., *Allies of a Kind: the United States, Britain and the War Against Japan, 1941–1945*, Clarendon Press, 1978.
137 Venkataramani, M. S. and Shrivastava, B. K., *Roosevelt, Gandhi, Churchill*, Sangam, 2nd edn, 1997.
138 Watt, D. C., *Succeeding John Bull: America in Britain's Place, 1900–1975*, Cambridge University Press, 1984.

THE SUEZ CRISIS OF 1956

139 Ashton, N. J., *Eisenhower, Macmillan and the Problem of Nasser*, Macmillan, 1996.
140 Beloff, M., 'The Crisis and Its Consequences for the British Conserva-tive Party' in Louis, W. R. and Owen, R. eds, *Suez 1956: The Crisis and Its Consequences*, Clarendon Press, 1989.
141 Campbell, J. C., 'The Soviet Union, the United States and the Twin Crises of Hungary and Suez' in Louis, W. R. and Owen, R. eds, *Suez 1956: The Crisis and Its Consequences*, Clarendon Press, 1989.
142 Carlton, D., *Anthony Eden*, Lane, 1981.
143 Carlton, D., *Britain and the Suez Crisis*, Blackwell, 1988.
144 Devereux, D. R., *The Formulation of British Defence Policy Towards the Middle East, 1948–56*, Macmillan, 1990.
145 Fullick, R. and Powell, G., *Suez: the Double War*, Hamish Hamilton, 1979.
146 Johnman, L., 'Defending the Pound: the Economics of the Suez Crisis, 1956' in Gorst, A., Johnman, L. and Lucas, W. S. eds, *Post-War Brit-ain, 1945–64: Themes and Perspectives*, Pinter Publishers, 1989.
147 Kent, J., 'The Egyptian Base and the Defence of the Middle East, 1945–54', *Journal of Imperial and Commonwealth History*, xxi, 1993.
148 Kunz, D. B., 'The Importance of Having Money: The Economic Diplo-macy of the Suez Crisis' in Louis, W. R. and Owen, R. eds, *Suez 1956: The Crisis and Its Consequences*, Clarendon Press, 1989.

149   Kyle, K., *Suez*, Weidenfield and Nicolson, 1991.
150   Lapping, B. and Low, D. A., 'Did Suez Hasten the End of Empire?',
      Contemporary Record, i, 1987.
151   Lucas, W. S., 'The Path to Suez: Britain and the Struggle for the Middle
      East, 1953–56' in Deighton, A. ed., *Britain and the First Cold War*,
      Macmillan, 1990.
152   Lucas, W. S., *Divided We Stand: Britain, the US and the Suez Crisis*,
      Hodder and Stoughton, 1991.
153   Lucas, W. S., 'A Most Peculiar War: Britain and the Suez Crisis',
      Modern History Review, vii, 1995.
154   Lucas, W. S. and Kakeyh, R., 'Alliance and Balance: the Anglo-Ameri-
      can Relationship and Egyptian Nationalism, 1950–57', *Diplomacy &
      Statecraft*, vii, 1996.
155   Mason, M., '"The Decisive Volley": the Battle of Ismailia and the
      Decline of British Influence in Egypt, January-July, 1952', *Journal of
      Imperial and Commonwealth History*, xix, 1991.
156   Rhodes James, R., *Anthony Eden*, Weidenfield and Nicolson, 1987.

OTHER DECOLONISATIONS

157   Ansprenger, F., *The Dissolution of the Colonial Empires*, Routledge,
      1989.
158   Betts, R. F., *France and Decolonisation, 1900–1960*, Macmillan, 1991.
159   Carrère d'Encausse, H., (translated by Philip, F.), *The End of the Soviet
      Empire: The Triumph of the Nations*, BasicBooks, 1993.
160   Chabal, P., 'Emergencies and Nationalist Wars in Portuguese Africa',
      Journal of Imperial and Commonwealth History, xxi, 1993.
161   Clarence-Smith, W. G., *The Third Portuguese Empire, 1825–1975: A
      Study in Economic Imperialism*, Manchester University Press, 1985.
162   Clayton, A., *The Wars of French Decolonization*, Longman, 1994.
163   Clayton, A., 'The End of Empire: The Experience of Britain and France
      and the Soviet Union/Russia Compared', *Strategic and Combat Stud-
      ies Institute*, Occasional Paper No. 17, 1995.
164   Groen, P. M. H., 'Militant Response: The Dutch Use of Military Force
      and the Decolonization of the Dutch East Indies, 1945–50', *Journal
      of Imperial and Commonwealth History*, xxi, 1993.
165   Holland, R. F., 'The Ends of Empire: Some Reflections on the
      Metropole', *The Round Table*, cccxvii, 1991.
166   Kent, J., *The Internationalization of Colonialism: Britain, France and
      Black Africa, 1939–1956*, Clarendon Press, 1992.
167   McCoy, A. W., 'The Philippines: Independence without Decolonisa-
      tion' in Jeffrey, R. ed., *Asia: The Winning of Independence*, Macmil-
      lan, 1981.
168   McMahon, R. J., *Colonialism and Cold War: The United States and
      the Struggle for Indonesian Independence, 1945–49*, Cornell Univer-
      sity Press, 1981.

169 MacQueen, N., *The Decolonization of Portuguese Africa*, Longman, 1996.

170 Marseille, J., 'The Phases of French Colonial Imperialism: Towards a New Periodization', *Journal of Imperial and Commonwealth History*, xiii, 1985.

171 Maxwell, K., 'Portugal and Africa: the Last Empire' in Gifford, P. and Louis, W. R. eds, *The Transfer of Power in Africa. Decolonization, 1940–1960*, Yale University Press, 1982.

172 Moore, B., 'Anglo-American Security Policy and its Threats to Dutch Colonial Rule in the West Indies, 1940–42', *Journal of Imperial and Commonwealth History*, xxiii, 1995.

173 Newitt, M., *Portugal in Africa*, Hurst, 1981.

174 Peemans, J-P., 'Imperial Hangovers: Belgium – The Economics of Decolonization', *Journal of Contemporary History*, xv, 1980.

175 Reid, A., 'Indonesia: Revolution without Socialism' in Jeffrey, R. ed., *Asia: The Winning of Independence*, Macmillan, 1981.

176 Smith, T., 'Patterns in the Transfer of Power: A Comparative Study of French and British Decolonization' in Gifford, P. and Louis, W. R. eds, *The Transfer of Power in Africa: Decolonization, 1940–1960*, Yale University Press, 1982.

177 Stengers, J., 'Precipitous Decolonization: The Case of the Belgian Congo' in Gifford, P. and Louis, W. R. eds, *The Transfer of Power in Africa: Decolonization, 1940–1960*, Yale University Press, 1982.

178 Wesseling, H. L., 'Post-Imperial Holland', *Journal of Contemporary History*, xv, 1980.

DOCUMENTARY SOURCES

179 Ashton, S. R. and Stockwell, S. E. eds, *Imperial Policy and Colonial Practice, 1925–1945*, 2 Volumes, HMSO, 1996.

180 Bridges, R. C., Dukes, P., Hargreaves, J. D. and Scott, W. eds, *Nations and Empires*, Macmillan, 1969.

181 De Silva, K. M. ed., *Sri Lanka*, 2 Volumes, HMSO, 1997.

182 Goldsworthy, D. ed., *The Conservative Government and the End of Empire, 1951–1957*, 3 Volumes, HMSO, 1994.

183 Gorst, A. and Johnman, L., *The Suez Crisis*, Routledge, 1997.

184 Hyam, R. ed., *The Labour Government and the End of Empire, 1945–1951*, 4 Volumes, HMSO, 1992.

185 Lucas, W.S., *Britain and Suez: The Lion's Last Roar*, Manchester University Press, 1996.

186 Mansergh, N. ed., *Constitutional Relations Between Britain and India: the Transfer of Power, 1942–1947*, 12 Volumes, HMSO, 1970–83.

187 Porter, A. N. and Stockwell, A. J., *British Imperial Policy and Decolonization, 1938–64*, 2 Volumes, Macmillan, 1987–9.

188 Rathbone, R. ed., *Ghana*, 2 Volumes, HMSO, 1992.

189 Stockwell, A. J. ed., *Malaya*, 3 Volumes, HMSO, 1995.

INDEX